Andy Thomas &

QUEST FOR CONTACT

A True Story of Crop Circles, Psychics and UFOs

29196

...tions

To the fond memory of Kim Besly

First published in 1997 by S.B. Publications
19 Grove Road, Seaford, East Sussex, BN25 1TP

All photographs & video images
by Andy Thomas unless otherwise stated

ISBN 1 85770 128 3

Typeset and printed by Island Press Ltd.
Tel: 01323 490222 UK

CONTENTS

Front & Back Cover / Title Page: *The sun touches the horizon, as watched from Wolstonbury Hill on the evening of 28th June 1995 (see Chapter 9).*

Inset Front Cover: *The crop formation at Felbridge which resulted from the Wolstonbury experiment (see chapter 10).*

ACKNOWLEDGEMENTS

The authors would like to thank everyone, listed alphabetically, who has been principally involved in the projects recounted in this book:

Steve Alexander, John Cole, Quenton Cole, Carole Coren, Adam Cotton, Karen Douglas, Michael Green, Martin Noakes, Jason Porthouse, Barry Reynolds, Linda Reynolds, David Russell, Diana Summer and Ted Richards.

Thanks also to:

Di Brown, Pauline Bura, Josie Cole, Griller Gilgannon, Mark Haywood, Tony Mezen, Sloane Noakes, Mark Porthouse, Danny Sotham, Heather Thomas, Ronald Thomas, Maureen and Lara at Colourfast, *everyone from Southern Circular Research/CCCS Sussex, BLT and Paul's Wednesday and Friday groups.*

Massive thanks to the following, who helped directly in the preparation of this book:

Stanley Messenger for his beautiful foreword.
John Holloway for specifically photographing Cissbury, Wolstonbury and Devil's Dyke.
Steve Benz for keeping the faith.
Debbie Pardoe for archaeological info on Wolstonbury and Cissbury.
Murry Hope for her unpublished contribution.
Carole Coren and *Diana Summer* for their blessings and memory-jogs.
Linda Reynolds for the photo opportunity.
Eve Branston for loan of video equipment.
Jason Porthouse for capturing the video images digitally onto disk, white line suggestion and motorcycle enthusiast omission.
Everyone who donated photographs and video images, credited in the captions.

And, of course...

Barry Reynolds for factual checking, investigative excursions and archive material.

Kaye Thomas for proof-reading, helpful suggestions and patience beyond the call of duty.

Thank you all.

"To have a full-blown taste for mystery one must take delight both in solving mysteries and in not solving them; in finding explanations for things and in living with things for which there currently is no explanation and which may be forever beyond explanation"

M SCOTT PECK

FOREWORD

BY STANLEY MESSENGER

This vibrant compact adventure story marks a crucial step on the evolving path of crop circle awareness. It actually does a lot more than that. It opens the door for a whole new generation of 'croppies' to reassess their own capacity to move beyond 'the paranormal' as an idea and into the situation where they too can cross the frontier into a different reality. Andy and Paul, by sharing both the pain of failure and the bliss of success on their quest for a different reality, have demonstrated that we can all begin to let go of the fear and uncertainty which are the main grounds for scepticism. On the frontier of the supersensible, sound judgement can never be based on fear. I quote Rudolf Steiner from one of his most powerful meditations: "*Steadfastly I set my Self into existence. Surefootedly I step forward upon the path of life*".

Having said that, it is also very necessary to breathe one's way out of the awe-struck solemnity and dogmatism which too easily takes hold when we first taste the heady wine of certainty. The paranormal dimension plays tricks. But it is useless to put up a defensive guard and tiptoe into the unknown world as if it were a minefield. Knowledge is a dance and reality is not our enemy. The humour in this book is not just a condiment, it is the very substance of the love which animates every step of the way. There is a great deal to love in this book. Andy doesn't parade his humility. His objectivity and persistence do this for him. And Paul is very courageous. He needs to be. But it is only too apparent that his polio is a very necessary factor in the process. It is *the* major obstacle that sharpens the attention of the participants on the need for continuity of awareness.

At the end of the day, what do we learn about reality in this story? Firstly we learn to take the end product, the crop circle itself, and, in fact, the whole phenomenal world, with a pinch of salt. Andy concludes not only that you can't prove anything, you don't actually need to because although the phenomenon is real it is not the whole reality. It only has the reality of a picture. Goethe concludes his *Faust* with the remark "*Everything transitory is no more than an appearance*" and goes on to say that what leads on into the real is what he calls "*the eternal feminine*". The Beings Andy and Paul contact in their quest speak naturally and spontaneously out of what they call *Ayesha*, the 'She' of Rider Haggard's Victorian occult romance. The female is the substance, the movement, the continuous event, out of which the repeated male forms arise, incarnated but transitory. So this is the second thing that this story tells us about the new real world we are going into at this millennial moment. The attention point is not the form, it is the event itself, the perpetually moving, evolving, cataclysmic event of the timeless, post-historical moment we are in. Events are Beings. Things, objects, are the essential pictures we need in order to be aware of the events, but they are transitory, mere pictures. Crop circles are hardly less transitory than UFOs. But they are pictures of the crucial Event of our time.

Is this then the whole story? Not quite, otherwise we would be permanently stuck in dualism - movement to form, form back into movement, never quite sure where the focus of reality lies. Crop circles are mysterious forms which bear witness to titanic cosmic and intimate human events. But the actual forms themselves lead beyond those events into realms which evoke thoughts, mathematical, creative, starry, which are no longer expressible in words. The Greeks simply called this Wisdom, and spoke of Kyriotetes, Lord of Wisdom, who stood permanently beyond both movement and form. Wisdom contains both the events and the facts which emerge from them.

There are tantalising hints in this story that the Beings, both in the elemental realm and among the Guardians whom Paul reaches, bear witness to this third realm, of which no being can yet speak, yet out of which everything, both in the events themselves and in the forms which sometimes emerge from them, ultimately springs.

STANLEY MESSENGER

Stanley Messenger is a leading philosopher in the world of crop circle research and a familiar figure at conferences in England and the USA. Over the years, Stanley has been many things including a medical student, actor, teacher in Rudolf Steiner schools, promoter of self-build housing and Family Violence Officer for Birmingham. Now retired, Stanley has found his true purpose, "aiding and abetting as many young people as possible to create their own reality and take responsibility for their own unique spiritual path".

"Crossing the frontier into a different reality..." 'Griller' Gilgannon drifts away in a crop formation, West Overton, Wiltshire, 1993.

Some of the people who play prominent roles in the following events...

Jason Porthouse

Karen Douglas

Barry Reynolds

Paul Bura

David Russell

Michael Green

Andy Thomas

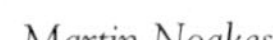

Martin Noakes

Linda Reynolds

Andy's first sight of a Sussex crop formation, Poynings, West Sussex, as seen from Devil's Dyke.

INTRODUCTION

by Andy Thomas

Fighting to keep the wheel from being yanked out of my hands by the strong gusts cutting across from the raging sea, I peered through the rain-spattered windscreen. The wipers were fighting valiantly to clear the glass but with little success. I turned into the street which would one day be so familiar to me but tonight was a mass of looming shapes behind a curtain of grey.

I had been here once before, but which house was it now? I remembered. The one with the decorative saucers, set into cement, covering the walls outside. I pulled in, up across the pavement as seemed to be the residents' tradition, and turned the engine off. I sat and thought for a while as the storm buffeted the car.

What had brought me here to Lancing in West Sussex on this apocalyptic August night? Crop circles, those shapes in the fields which seemed to change the lives of so many, they were the culprits. My honeymoon with Kaye in Wiltshire the year before had given me my first taste of crop formations. I knew from the media that these strange patterns appeared there and I had been quietly looking out for them although I didn't really know why. On the last morning before our return home, an inner urge made me ask our bed and breakfast hostess if there were any crop circles nearby. She instantly produced a map and pointed out the roads from where we would be able to see the latest enigmatic designs. In that moment, although I didn't know it then, my destiny had been reshaped.

Later that morning, on the Marlborough downs, I caught my first hazy glimpse of a crop pattern in the distance, and I was hooked. It was as if this was the missing piece in my life for which I had been waiting but didn't know until it was there in front of me. I walked around in a daze for the rest of that day, frantically searching for the next formation and being knocked out by the scale and complexity of those I encountered and the questions they raised. What had made them? What did they mean?

On our homecoming to Sussex on the south-east coast, I was eager to tell everyone about the incredible shapes we had witnessed. In my enthusiasm I was a little taken aback by some of the scepticism and indifference I met in the eyes of friends. Matthew, an old school mate, didn't seem too impressed. After all, crop circles were everywhere - hadn't I seen the one at Poynings in West Sussex? Two hours later, we were standing at the car park of the ancient landmark Devil's Dyke, north of Brighton, looking down at what he had found. A simple dumbbell shape lay below us, clear and precise. Matthew was convinced it was the work of jokers. I wasn't so sure, especially after some of the vaster, more complex designs I had walked in the week before.

When the Doug and Dave news story broke the next month, two old men claiming they had created all of the crop formations with nothing more than rope and planks, Matthew rang to see if I had heard the news. I bought a copy of the newspaper with the headline screamer "THE MEN WHO CONNED THE WORLD" and sat, head spinning, in the sun on Brighton seafront to digest the implications. Could I and many others really have been fooled so easily into thinking the crop circles were of some unexplained origin when all it was were two retired pranksters having a laugh? As I considered the article, I rapidly came to the conclusion, as did many others across the country, that the story didn't add up. There were too many patterns, too huge and precise and with too many anomalous effects to be created in the way the tabloid would have us believe. Doug and Dave couldn't possibly be responsible for what they were claiming. I decided then and there to discover for myself more about this mysterious phenomenon.

The next few months (to Kaye's dismay) were a blur of intense, almost obsessive research, searching for every book, every article, every scrap I could about crop circles. I couldn't sleep some nights, so excited was I by what I was unearthing. Here was a modern mystery that most certainly wasn't anything to do with pensioners and planks of wood. At the back of one of the books I found an address for an organisation called the Centre for Crop Circle Studies (CCCS). I was a member within a month.

Towards the end of 1991 I was contacted by Barry Reynolds. He was gathering together CCCS members in East or West Sussex to form a local branch to investigate crop circles which appeared within the Sussex borders. In December our branch held its inaugural meeting and I found myself volunteering to edit a newsletter, the *Sussex Circular,* which would rapidly develop into a monthly venture and become known world-wide by its initials SC.

From the seven people who turned up for the first meeting at Burgess Hill Scout Centre, our numbers grew rapidly until thirty or more were gathering each month to find out the latest news from the fields. One regular attender seemed particularly charismatic. Wearing a pope-like skull cap and smock and carrying a distinctive gnarled walking stick, most of the time he would sit quietly at the back with a young male companion (his nephew Quenton, it turned out), absorbing the information being given out. But when he spoke, his deep booming tones and presence filled the room, turning every head. This man was Paul Bura. And through my future friendship with Paul astonishing things, which began that stormy night in Lancing, were to happen over the next three years which would irrevocably change the lives of more than just ourselves...

This book records those extraordinary events and tells the story of how a group of us got together to try and discover what was behind the crop circle phenomenon and to gather evidence for its authenticity by using psychic information as our guide, for better or worse. Our work began as an attempt to video a crop pattern forming but turned into something much deeper. By the end of our journey, many of us would be transformed by some of the incredible phenomena we witnessed and some of the insights we received.

Everything that follows happened exactly as described, with no exaggeration or distortion. Thus our successes - as well as our failures - are recounted together in chronological order. The task of Paul and I has been to preserve the atmosphere, passion and humour of the times we all spent together, to capture the magic of those experiences.

We hope that our exploits and achievements will encourage others to reach inside themselves to discover hidden depths and talents which they can utilise and develop and that the questions raised by the events described inspire people to look at the world around them with new eyes. Our exploits revealed to us, at least, that the Universe is indeed a magical place where most things are possible if not always predictable.

Conventional science tells us that some of the events in the following chapters can't happen. Those trained only in the scientific method will think our exploits and musings self-delusional. This is not a book for them. And yet it throws down a challenge to science to accept that what appears to be outside its realms *may* one day be explained within them, without resorting to accusing those who witness such things of being deranged or liars. Our experiences suggest that many levels of existence intertwine and that cause and effect is much more than just a physical process.

This book touches on difficult subjects which are hard to prove to sceptical minds - yet we are not setting out to prove anything. If the reader doesn't adhere to the belief-systems outlined and utilised in the course of our work, we ask only that it be accepted that these were the paths *WE* chose to tread. They don't exclude the potential truths of other directions. Whatever view taken, the resulting story should prove of interest to all drawn to 'the paranormal' (ie. that which simply isn't understood yet) and gives a valuable insight into the lives of those who spend their time investigating and attempting to interact with forces beyond our day-to-day experience.

Much of the book, as the subtitle suggests, concerns crop circles and makes reference to psychic channelling, yet this is not intended as a comprehensive guide to either and we refer readers to other sources for general background information.

Briefly, for newcomers, crop circles are the strange patterns of spiralled stems found etched into agricultural meadows each summer. Documentation appears to reveal they have been appearing on and off for the last few centuries, but since the early 1980's they have blossomed in numbers, complexity and geographical distribution to the point where they are now a global phenomenon and hundreds are discovered each year in England alone, which remains the centre of activity. Many reports of strange phenomena surround their appearance, including accounts and recordings of anomalous lights and unusual sounds. There is much debate as to their origins and meaning. Amongst the many options, some believe extra-terrestrial forces are at work, others say unknown natural forces are responsible and sceptics claim secret landscape artists are to blame. This book explores one path of possibilities.

Psychic channelling or 'mediumship' is a gift recorded throughout history and many cultures in wise men, shamens and religious figures. It appears to enable spiritual entities from different dimensions and worlds to speak through human beings, most commonly by their use of the channeller's vocal chords although other methods can be used. There is nothing evil or 'occult' about it. It seems to work by the medium raising their 'vibrational frequency' and by the entity lowering its own, meeting somewhere in the middle, allowing interaction to take place. Like crop circles, this is a controversial subject, inviting much scepticism from some and many questions about its origins. Some believe the characters who come through are who they claim to be, others assert they are simply the subconscious mind of the channeller being accessed. Whatever the case, there is clearly a real phenomenon here which is beyond fraud (in most cases) and opens discussion about the untapped powers of the human mind. There is an increasing number of ordinary folk out there practising channelling and uncannily accurate and useful information has been forthcoming on occasion, though it is not always reliable as we would discover in our own work.

Our years of communication experiments all took place in the beautiful landscape of our home counties East and West Sussex. Throughout the story, reference is made to some of the crop formations which have appeared here but in general details on these are kept to a minimum and the only ones mentioned are those which were pertinent to our work. For a comprehensive guide to the many patterns which have appeared in Sussex over the years, including more technical information on the ones referred to here, my previous book *Fields Of Mystery* fills in the gaps and also includes a chapter on the wider history of the circle phenomenon. (In turn, that book very briefly touches on the incredible events recounted here.) See the appendices for more details.

Finally, a word about how this book is presented. Splitting duties between two writers raises the difficult question of how to collate the results. In the interests of allowing the text and story to flow, I am responsible for the binding narrative which leads the book and Paul's contributions are dropped in as quotes throughout the text.

Despite my involvement with the projects this story recounts, I remain completely open-minded as to the source and purpose of the mysterious crop glyphs. Our work as a team was always about exploring possibilities and each of the participants took their own view of the events and their significance. For some, it provided the ultimate answer as to what is behind the crop circles. To others, the phenomenon remains a mystery and the experiments were about trying to shed light on certain aspects of it. Equally, the reader must make up his or her own mind about the ultimate implications of our quest for contact with hitherto unreachable forces.

INTRODUCTION

by Paul Bura

I was standing behind the counter of our health food shop in Lancing, West Sussex, writing out cheques for various suppliers. In the background, as usual, Radio 4 poured forth its daily content of news, current affairs and drama. And then... "*...the city has been hit by a huge earthquake measuring 6.8 on the Richter scale. Hundreds are feared dead. This is the end of this news flash.*" My head jerked upward. "What the hell was that?" I said out loud. "What city? Where?" In the time it took to walk to the bottom of the stairs to call my sister Josie I remember thinking: Joeb talked about forthcoming Earth changes. Surely not yet! "Josie, did you hear that?" She came out of the living room and stood at the top of the stairs. "Hear what?" she said. "Can't I have my lunch in peace?" I replied: "That news flash. The earthquake, the city, hundreds dead!" I was almost angry that she hadn't heard it. She MUST have heard it. "We'll check the next main bulletin at three o'clock," she said and walked back to complete her lunch. The news came and went. Nothing! Four o'clock, five o'clock. Nothing! I must have been really losing it. The TV news gave forth nothing. The next day, Sunday, came and went. Nothing in the newspapers, nothing via radio and TV. Monday morning I came down for breakfast. The newspaper headlines: 'MASSIVE EARTHQUAKE HITS CAIRO. HUNDREDS DEAD.' The earthquake measured 6.8 on the Richter scale!

Years before, just outside my home town of Herne Bay in Kent, I had finished visiting an old friend of mine, Will Combes. As I got into my car another vehicle pulled up at a turning just up on the right from where I was parked. I recognised the occupants as very close friends of mine: Colin (who was driving), Christine (a young French girl), Gary and Martin. I sounded the horn and waved. They didn't see me. They pulled round past me and I could clearly see Christine leaning over the back seat talking to Martin. They were all, including myself, students of the well-known medium Gladys Franklin, and I had intended to visit her after seeing Will. It was obvious that Colin and the others were on their way there also. They, after all, *lived* with Gladys. I started the car and hared off after them. I caught them up on the brow of a hill and could see Martin and Gary laughing and talking through the back window. I flashed my lights, waved, hooted the horn. They didn't seem to see or hear. We came to a T-Junction: to the right was Herne Bay, to the left was the house where Gladys Franklin lived. I expected them to turn left; they turned right! I imagined they were going to Herne Bay to do some shopping. I gave one last toot on the horn, turned left and drove off to see Gladys.

I was there in no time. I parked the car and crunched my way up the gravel path, knocked on the door and waited. The door opened and there stood... "Colin," I said, very startled. "What the hell are you doing here?" I knew that what I was saying was utterly stupid because he replied "Well I *live* here, Paul." "B... b... but I've just seen you and Christine, Gary and Martin in the car. I followed you down the road I..." "We've been in all afternoon," said Colin, smiling, "and you know that Christine is in Gibraltar!" "Well I *know* she's in Gibraltar," I replied "But if I've just SEEN her in the car then she ISN'T, is she?" I was almost hysterical. "I think you'd better come in," said Colin. I staggered into the kitchen where Gary and Martin were having a cup of tea with Gladys. It was then that I realised that Colin, Christine, Gary and Martin would leave her forever within six months. This was what my vision had meant. I knew it was an incredible event to be witness to and part of, a three-dimensional drama that was as real as this word processor and all I got out of it was the knowledge that these people would depart Gladys for good. The fact is, that was exactly what they did.

Such visions or premonitions have punctuated my life throughout. With them always comes insight and direction.

I first met Andy Thomas after a customer of mine, John Cole (a teacher of maths and science and a fellow follower of the mystic life), suggested I attend a meeting held by the Sussex branch of the Centre for Crop Circle Studies. I said that I would and after John had reminded me a couple of times, I made my way to Burgess Hill to attend a meeting held there at the Scout Centre. Something told me that doing so was very important. I didn't think that it would change my life. But a deep prompting, over and above those of John, urged me on and my nephew Quenton and I attended our first meeting. Crop circles fascinated me. Those amazingly powerful symbols in the corn clutched at my inner being. This was not an emotional response but a spiritual one. Andy always spoke with great enthusiasm and zeal. I noticed that he could never keep still, his slim body, dressed always in black, twisted this way and that expressing the excitement that this subject stimulated in him. During the interval Andy was handing out copies of *SC*. He approached me, magazine in hand. "Do you want one?" he said. "Yes please," I replied. "Are you a subscriber?" said Andy. "No," I said. "Well you can't have one then." I laughed. The bond was made. I liked his style.

Later I gave a talk and demonstration on dowsing. After the talk an Ordnance Survey map was plonked down in front of me and I was asked by Barry Reynolds and Andy to see if I could dowse where the next crop formation would appear. "The bastards!" I thought. "And in front of all these people. Oh well, better get on with it." This was my first tentative step in working with a group of people who were to become very special to me.

My whole life has been a quest, a quest for truth. Often events knocked on my door and entered without asking. Now I was doing the knocking. Another quest of mystery had begun. I got more than I could dare dream!

The house of the saucers; Paul's home at Lancing.

1: THE HOUSE OF THE SAUCERS

The ancient church stood where it had for centuries, lit dimly with a pallor of deathly orange from the glow of its modern neighbouring settlement. A silence hung in the air, broken only by the occasional roar from the nearby road. The temple could feel the lines of power which throbbed through its body, rushing down from its even more ancient predecessor a few miles north-west. The energy splayed and radiated out from its walls like rays of light. Suddenly a sense of urgency filled its umbilical line. It felt a surge of light pass through its stones and the earth beneath it, reaching out on one of the rays to the field nearby. In the field, the air was disturbed. Stalks of green wheat, each one a living entity, instantly lay down as if on command, spiralling in a vortex.

A day passed. The sun rose and continued its arc across the sky until it fell once more. In the hours of light a few eyes were turned toward the field to witness the wonder which had arrived there, but a few only. As the orange-tinged darkness returned, so again did a surge of light through the land, the church, the field. More stems obeyed the order to lay. On this night a symbol was born to accompany its circular companion and when the sun again began its ascent, this time more eyes were drawn to the extraordinary sight which greeted them.

The New Arrival

The crop formation which appeared at Sompting, West Sussex, on the nights of June 24th and 25th 1992 was not the first of its kind to arrive in the area - a 'pictogram' had been found in 1990 as the crop circle phenomenon began its first leap into complex symbolism - but it was the first to provide the trigger in a group of people for what was to become a four-year odyssey of metaphysical exploration. A circle arrived the first night and a pattern of radiating arches the next, overlooking the seaside metropolis of Lancing, Sompting and Worthing from a field north of the busy A27 road.

The pictogram at Sompting, 1992, which was to be the inspiration for so much... Photo: David Russell

The old Knights Templar church of St Mary's which stood directly to the south-east of the field already had a history of mystical significance and an aura of the occult about it, stemming from the old forbidden wisdom of the persecuted Templars who had made the church their own in the twelfth century. A crop circle so close to the old temple wasn't out of place with the location's demeanour.

St Mary's church, Sompting, the centre of much crop circle activity over the years.

As the formation gazed out south across the nearby estates, it attracted the attention of a group of people who had already dedicated themselves to learning more about this incredible phenomenon. The Centre for Crop Circle Studies, Sussex branch, had been created at the end of 1991 and some of its members in the region were already lying in wait for the bizarre and beautiful symbols to revisit their homeland.

Two brothers who shared a passion to know more about the circles had gone one step further than waiting - in an unintentional joint request, they openly invited the circle-making forces to do their work in the Sompting area. On 23rd June, Mark and Jason Porthouse, without knowing what the other was doing, had taken themselves out to two separate locations to sit and think. Mark stood on the hill behind St Mary's and, out loud, not really sure who he was talking to, asked "Why can't we have a crop circle here?". Simultaneously, a mile or so north, Jason found himself at the entrance to the east embankment of Cissbury Ring, an ancient Iron Age hill-fort, and also made a request that the crop circles visit the area. In the early hours of the next morning, their plea was answered and the gates had been opened to a series of extraordinary events. Less than a month later, Mark and Jason would attend a gathering which would have a profound effect on the lives of everyone present.

Paul serves a customer in his health-food store, an unofficial gathering place for the metaphysically-minded.

Enter The Psychic

One acquaintance the Porthouse brothers had made was that of local shopkeeper Paul Bura who ran a health food store in the high street at Lancing. The quaintly old-fashioned shop, which smelt charmingly of herbs and wood, had become a little meeting place for those interested not only in buying a pound of organic potatoes and a slice of home-made pie but also in questioning the nature of the world around them. Paul, disabled by polio as a child, had developed the gift of psychic mediumship over the years, yet only a few of his closer customers were treated to this intriguing information. His friendly and open demeanour seemed to trigger conversations about 'life, the universe and everything' as a matter of course. Paul had recently been talking about crop circles with one of his customers, John Cole, a founder member of CCCS Sussex. When Jason told him of the formation which had just appeared less than a mile from Lancing, and that the farmer was amenable to CCCS visitors, Paul knew he had to find out more:

"Jason and Mark, their mother Sylvia and father Steven, were regular customers of mine. All were interested in the paranormal and the brothers were brought up in an atmosphere of acceptance and freedom of thought. We talked on every subject pertaining to 'other worlds', healing, dowsing, dreams and mediumship. At that time I had not told anyone in any real detail of my gift of channelling. When Jason told me that a crop formation had gone down near St Mary's church at Sompting I knew I had to see it. I asked whether it was possible to get me into the formation. We could drive most of the way but there was an iron gate across the private road owned by the farmer. From there it would have to be a 'wheelchair job'. Jason and Quenton were convinced it was no problem and within two days we were ready. I had made an Egyptian Cross or ankh from a piece of thick wire. In earlier experiments I had once heard of at

Stonehenge, an ankh cross made of wire had been waved over the stones. The result was that some kind of energy literally threw the holder of the cross several feet in the air and paralysed his arm. It was six months before he fully recovered. What we were going to investigate was a crop formation but I felt similar energies were at play here and I wanted to see whether I could tap it. Being a polio person since the age of seven I knew what paralysis was and I wasn't in the market for more. But when I get an idea in my head I *have* to give it a try."

"It was a Wednesday afternoon and it had been raining between the sunshine. We took umbrellas just in case. The formation was just off the A27 near an old chalk pit. We had to drive up a small secluded road until we reached the iron gate. From there the lads hauled out the wheelchair. We were off. I remember feeling very excited but also apprehensive, not because of the ankh cross that I was clutching to my bosom but the physical problem of actually getting into the formation. We came to the edge of the field. The boys hauled me out of the chair. Quenton started to lead me like a blind man through the tram lines of the field, my left hand clamped firmly onto his right shoulder, my right hand, knuckles white, gripping my beloved old alder stick. Jason went ahead of us holding the wheelchair shoulder-high. Slowly we made our, for me, treacherous, snail-like way to this, my first crop formation. I wanted to get to it so badly, yet I couldn't hurry if I wanted to. One false move and I would go down like a felled tree, not only damaging myself but the crop. I was sweating now and breathing hard."

Inside the maze of the pictogram at Sompting. St Mary's church can be seen at the foot of the hill.

"Suddenly, there it was! A work of art way above any basket that I had seen woven. It was in two sections. "Get me into the middle of the larger one," I asked, almost demanded. The wheelchair was placed plumb centre of the largest of these two beauties. I sat and closed my eyes. I could feel the energy around me; I was in the middle of a whirling vortex of power. Suddenly my psychic mind saw a tall figure with a long flowing beard carrying a huge scythe. I knew that this was merely symbolic of the energy contained within this incredible pattern etched into the corn. There was something here, something that I had never experienced before in all my life. This was real! But who would believe it? Strangely this was the first of only two formations that I have ever physically entered. My task, I was to find out much later, was to do with the mind. Entering too many circles would detach me from the job I was destined to do, maybe not a great job but one that I was proud to be a part of."

"I took out the ankh cross and very gingerly scanned around me. I could feel something akin to static run up my arm, but very gentle. As the cross arced toward the direction of St Mary's church I felt a surge of energy. Arcing away again it lessened in power. I again brought it in the direction of the church; again the surge of energy. I knew then that there was a connection between the circle and St Mary's. Later, after map dowsing the area I realised that an energy line came from Cissbury Ring, a well-known earth energy centre, and passed through the church. From here, a line connected to the circle."

The impressive size of the Sompting formation wasn't apparent until inside it...

Earth Energy & Dowsing

The energy line which came from Cissbury was one of many which we would discover in the coming years. The idea of 'earth energy' is now commonly accepted amongst psychics and 'dowsers'. As acupuncturists believe the human body is covered in 'meridian' lines of *ch'i*, so many believe the planet itself is networked by complex strips of energy possibly formed from piezoelectric fields generated by moving water and geophysical pressure in rocks and crystals. Although modern science denies its existence, some hold that ancient man knew how to locate this force and erected temples and stone sarsens to mark and focus specific power points, often where lines crossed. Dowsers claim that crop circles nearly always appear at similar places of energy concentration which is perhaps why they often seem to proliferate around prehistoric sites. 'Dowsing' is an old art which, with the aid of rods and pendulums, seems to be able to detect not only earth energy and, most commonly, water, but also objects and even places using maps, by asking the dowsing implement to move yes or no when asked questions. Through this, by a process of elimination, a successful answer can result. Quite *how* this works is not really understood but the fact that oil companies are known to regularly employ such methods is testimony to the simple fact that it *can* work although it is not always reliable and much depends on the experience of the individual as Paul explains:

"There appears to be a vast reservoir of knowledge of all things past, present and, to an extent, future. All human beings are connected psychically to this cosmic computer which can be accessed by most people using the tools of the dowser's trade. The ancients called this 'reservoir' the Akashic Record. Everything that is has its own frequency. All a human being has to do is tune in to that frequency simply by asking. But it still takes hours, if not years, of practice, trial and error. A good psychic/dowser needs no tools whatsoever, just a focused, receptive mind into which sound and pictures can be received and information given. Another name for this phenomenon is the Universal Overself."

Through dowsing, we would later discover more about the energy lines which covered the local countryside and Cissbury Ring would later give us the setting for one of the greatest moments of the project that was about to be born. As Paul, Quenton and Jason departed from the Sompting crop formation, they were in a state of euphoria:

"It was time to leave. The elemental forces held off the rain just long enough for us to vacate the field. I felt good. We *all* felt good. Quenton took charge of the wheelchair. We hurtled back to the iron gate at full throttle, Quenton jumping on the back of the chair as we free-wheeled together down the sloping gradient, nearly smashing into the gate. "Wow," I thought. "So this is what it's about!" The rain came then and I didn't care."

Tea In The House Of Saucers

Soon after this experience, John Cole invited Paul to one of the monthly CCCS Sussex meetings, where he instantly made an impression on many of those present, with his tales of dowsing and psychic communication. Paul and I were drawn together in conversation and I soon found myself drinking tea one evening, deep in a dialogue of universal contemplation, in the converted loft of the bungalow where he lived with his mother. Sitting in a road just set back from Lancing seafront, their home was distinguished by the collection of decorative saucers adhered to its front. Little did we realise that this house and the small upper lounge with its tiny kitchenette would come to mean so much to so many in the years to come.

As we talked, Paul spoke about his experiences in the Sompting formation and outlined a plan he had to discover more about its origins. A group of his friends were meeting the following week for a meditation to contemplate the pattern which had appeared so close by. Would I like to come? I knew hardly anything about meditation but was fascinated with the idea, though I couldn't see, in my naiveté, how this could lead to information. Nevertheless, fatefully, I agreed to attend.

The room where most of our psychic communications were to take place over the years, upstairs at Paul's.

The First Communication

On the evening of August 13th 1992, one of the worst gales that year hit the south coast of England. With the sea crashing on the front, black cloud looming and rain lashing horizontally in frightening winds, a number of people made their treacherous way to the house of the saucers.

For this meeting a group of ten or so gathered around the large wooden table in the downstairs dining room, lit by candles. Each attender was a friend or acquaintance of Paul; some knew each other, others didn't, but everyone seemed friendly. Those present were the ones Paul felt were right for the particular aims of the evening. On the central oak table, in front of each person was a photocopied illustration of the formation at Sompting which had prompted this gathering, and some corn from the field. The group would hold the image in their minds to see if any enlightening thoughts would arise from the subconscious as to what the crop circles were about and what the minds (if any) behind them wanted from humanity. Paul recalls:

"The weather on that August evening was horrendous. The elements of wind, rain and hail took their turns in battering my small home as if to try and scare the folk present before we'd even started. Not only that but the date on that seemingly fateful day was the 13th... it was also a full moon. The moon had always been my 'friend' and as a professional writer and performer of poetry it had always given me inspiration. I wasn't afraid of the moon. As for the weather, that didn't disturb me either; I LOVED it. The drama of nature was of great moment to me, so I was happy to let it roar."

At 8.00pm, with the storm hammering the window outside, the candles were put out and the group sat in silence and semi-darkness, turning the Sompting symbol over and over in their minds. In thought, the crop patterns are freed from their two-dimensional cage and they can be twisted and turned in three-dimensional beauty. Many believe

The downstairs room where the very first group communication from 'Joeb' was received one tempestuous August night.

what we are seeing in our fields are simply flat representations of multi-dimensional energies and that we need to explore the designs in this way to unlock their secrets further.

Suddenly Paul's breathing increased rapidly and his posture changed. In the gloom, I could just see that his facial muscles were being unnaturally stretched as if they were taking on a new persona. Those who had never witnessed the like of what was about to occur looked up, startled. A voice suddenly cut through the groan of the wind outside, dry and ancient, quiet but commanding. Although I had known of Paul's 'gifts', I hadn't realised until then just what 'getting information' entailed. Now I knew; this was what would have once been called a seance. The voice, speaking through Paul's vocal chords, delivered a disturbing message...

"The circles are just the beginning, planted for Man to make him think... or to make him scoff. The weather... strange. There will be much more. Man will be forced to know of what is to pass. Do not listen to those who scoff because within you, you know. This is very important; the true self. 'The signs of the times' you've heard it said - THESE are the signs of the times! But this is nothing. Nature is supreme, so powerful, so awe-inspiring, you would die. But she is gentle, and she has always been so. Man has made her angry; she is in pain. She is crying for help and you CAN help. You have work to do. I have seen the Spirit of the Earth in all her beauty. She would dazzle you, brilliant and wonderful. I am privileged to bask in this. Look within yourselves, you will find her there. There will be damage done along this coastline; a little bit here; a little bit there. Questions will be asked. Some will scoff. But you must not despair."

With these last words, Paul's breathing quietened again and all was still. His face was once again his own. Nobody said a word, stunned. Paul describes the experience from his perspective:

"Andy hadn't the foggiest idea what to expect. I had news for him: I didn't know either! Incense was swirling around the room like fog and candles were in profusion. I explained our mission was to appeal to the Earth Spirit (Gaia) to help us to understand the crop circle enigma in the hope that one or more of us would pick up information on a psychic/spiritual level. I had no idea that what was about to happen would change my life forever."

"I gave an invocation and as the candles flickered and the weather howled in seeming defiance, we settled into silence. I had no intention of channelling; clairvoyance maybe. I cleared my mental screen ready for whatever pictures and information should come my way. Nothing happened. *Then suddenly there it was:* that familiar tingle up and down my arms and over my face. My breathing started to become laboured and rhythmic. "I'm going into channelling mode," I thought. "This is not what I expected. Better go with it." My aspect began to change as another entity drew near and was imprinting itself onto my personality, using facial muscles in a way that I never did. I could stop this any time I wanted to. But I didn't want to stop it, I had to let go to IT, whatever or whoever it was. The words started to tumble out, at first slow and laborious, then they quickened in pace and passion. Here was a personality of strength and dignity. I *liked* this man, whoever he was. His words were dramatic and apocalyptic, yet beautiful in their simplicity. But it was strong stuff. I'm told that his voice rolled and skated over the elemental sounds outside, a back-drop that compelled one to listen. He left me then, leaving me bewildered and a little scared. Scared not because of him but of what he said. I knew that at the end of every millennium the prophets came out of the woodwork and the doom-merchants came into their own. But what this being had told us was not all doom but full of light and wisdom, strength and hope and an identification with the Earth Mother that literally blew our minds!"

When the lights were turned back on and the group were treated to hot soup in what would become an ongoing ritual, they talked about the significance of the message. We didn't know then the source of the communication but were aware that other mediums or 'channellers' had received similarly portentous discourses, talk of 'Earth changes' which would bring initial destruction to parts of the planet but ultimate harmony. Were the crop circles the harbingers of such events? The voice had seemed to think so. Everyone agreed that the experiment should be repeated and that the communicator needed to be contacted again in an attempt to clarify the meaning of his message. With this decision, a regular meditation group was born and many of those who had gathered on this stormy night would come together again each week to discover more.

Joeb

As time went by, the communicator returned and told us more of who and what he was. He called himself 'Joeb' (pronounced *Jobe*), and claimed to be a "*discarnate human being*" who had lived many lives on Earth but currently resided in an existence between "*the fourth and fifth dimension*". He retained the persona of a Burmese wiseman from the 16th century, his last earthly incarnation, and now acted in the service of Gaia (or 'Ayesha' as he would later call her), the Earth Mother. There seemed little to do for the moment but accept him at face value. Whether or not Joeb was who he said he was or if this was some strange part of Paul's subconscious mind producing archetypal characters to dispense hidden information seemed irrelevant. Here was a persona which could be conversed with. Paul channelled Joeb not in some drab monotone voice, but as a huge personality full of wit, wisdom and passion. Eventually, he was to discover that Joeb had spoken through him once before:

"It was four years later that Joeb told me it was he I had channelled once *six years before* in Herne Bay, Kent when I was sitting with a group of three. He spoke then about *"Vast Earth changes"*. This small group of which I was a part had been told previously, by psychic means, that a being would be coming to speak with us in three weeks time. When that time arrived it was also a full moon. Again, I was chosen to be the mouthpiece. After the entity had spoken, my good friend Malcolm uttered the words that I shall never forget: "Paul, it's utter bollocks!" "Malcolm," I answered, "who knows."

The Circles Explained?

After the gloomy nature of Joeb's first message, he brightened considerably as the essence of whatever he was learnt to communicate more fully. He began to come through more loudly and positively and, we soon realised, had a sense of humour. His essential message was the same though - the crop circles were the first outward signs that big changes were on the way. They were appearing, he said, to attract the attention of those who had incarnated specifically to help the planet through a difficult time of transformation. They were like beacons to awaken minds to the task ahead of them, the symbolism containing information which could be accessed through the intellect but worked mostly on the subconscious. The circles were created by a combination of extra-terrestrial intelligences, Devic forces (nature spirits) and the consciousness of the Earth Mother herself. Paul elaborates on Joeb's explanation of how the crop glyphs worked:

"One thing Joeb always made clear was the power contained in shape. He would illustrate this by describing the meditative powers of 'mandalas', complex but beautiful patterns drawn on the basis of a circle but with intricate interweaving of line, colour and geometry. If one contemplated these visual aids the inner mind could access a higher form of consciousness beyond the third dimension. These shapes, such as sacred mazes, are etched into the ground all over the Earth, many still to be found in England at various stately homes. When one walks one of these, one enters a meditative state."

"Andy and I once constructed such a maze using chalk and a large piece of black paper. A group of us took our shoes off and slowly walked the intricate path until we reached the middle. By then we were, without doubt, 'energised', light-headed and tingling. In order to 'switch off' that energy we had to re-trace our steps. I say 'we'. Actually, because of the polio thing, I could not attempt this. Instead, I pointed my finger at the beginning of the maze and slowly followed the path with my eye and mind. By the time I had reached the destined middle section, I too was in a calm, warm, meditative state. Although I knew about shape power long before I met Joeb, it made so much sense to me when he told us that the complex and stunningly beautiful shapes, drawn so exquisitely by the circle-making forces, were there to *"open the minds of men, that he might understand"*.

The huge and beautiful megaliths at mysterious Avebury, Wiltshire. Many believe ancient sites like these hold very strong 'earth energies'.

"Many of these extraordinary creations acted as triggers on the subconscious. Andy, to name but one person, saw a crop circle and his life was changed forever. Joeb claimed that many, not all, were ancient symbols of power and coded information put down into the earth energy grid aeons ago, now being reactivated. All of the genuine circles had water underneath them and were joined by powerful lines of energy, leading to local ancient energy sites such as Cissbury Ring, Avebury in Wiltshire and the Rollright Stones in Oxfordshire."

Joeb's messages fitted a pattern which had been recorded by other seers and channellers, with talk of the Earth shifting on its axis within our lifetimes and of great physical and spiritual changes to come. Earthquakes, fire and flood would come but it would not be the end of the world, just a positive kick in the pants for humanity - although there was a chance this future could be averted, the lessons learned without destruction if enough heads could be turned in time. Humankind needed to transform itself spiritually and socially. The energy grid of the planet was trying to convert itself into a 'higher frequency' but the negativity being psychically generated from our collective blackness was being poured into the planet through endless engagement in war, prejudice and our insistence on polluting the environment, and the Earth was responding in kind. Thus we were partly bringing about the destructive aspect of the changes ourselves. A step back from our malaise could prevent the worst of what was being predicted. The crop circles were a part of our awakening to this realisation, as Paul clarifies:

"These things had come about, according to Joeb, because the Earth Mother's frequency was changing. We were slowly going from a 'three-dimensional vibration' to a 'four-dimensional' one. Even time appeared to be speeding up. In addition to humankind's negative outpourings into the energy grid, part of the reaction to this higher and faster frequency would be strange weather conditions: more hurricanes, drought, floods, disease, volcanic upheaval, plus personal spiritual conflict. This new frequency, of which the circles were representative, would repel those who did not wish to make this leap into higher consciousness. Joeb told us that all would be given the choice to make it or not and that JUDGEMENT WAS NOTHING TO DO WITH IT. We all had free-will, the choice would be ours. He said that our 'karma' (the law of cause and effect and personal debt) would be worked out elsewhere in the Universe if we decided not to take that leap of consciousness here."

Apocalypse Now?

In the first few weeks this information came through, it certainly had a huge effect on those hearing it. Some of us would drive around in shock trying to visualise our favourite towns underwater, the earth moving underneath our feet and the sky spinning as the planet tilted... After a while, some would take their own view on Joeb's words. In any case, they were less a prophecy, more a warning of what *could* happen. There was the danger that if too many people around the world expected change of a disastrous kind then they might precipitate it themselves with their actions and the resultant energy they generated into the Earth's grid. All we could do was stop worrying and wait and see.

Although some believe such portents from all number of sources are simply twisted New Age nonsense and misplaced end-of-the-millennium scaremongering, Joeb's words in particular seemed to have a resonance with many people's personal views, and he spoke with a sense of humanity and love missing from some channelled communications. Joeb's views soon made their way into print in a variety of journals and quite without plan transcriptions of his conversations began to be distributed widely by underground networks which kept tabs on all the latest channelled information from various mediums. Eventually they reached the attention of Michael Green, the then Chairman of the main Centre for Crop Circle Studies, and a sequence of extraordinary events was set into motion.

"There will be damage done along this coastline..." Would the seas rise to cover Sussex?

Devil's Dyke, north of Brighton, centre of the psychic vision Paul was to receive for our first rendezvous experiment. Photo: John Holloway

2: THE QUEST BEGINS

Shades of Green

The Centre for Crop Circle Studies had been formed in 1990 to investigate the proliferating phenomenon of the beautiful shapes visiting the crop fields of England. As the patterns spread out across the world in a big way, so the CCCS and its profile grew. At the helm of this organisation was a tall, distinctive character with a pleasantly Victorian air about him; Michael Green. As Chairman he was loved and respected by many as the 'right man for the job' even if his authoritarian style of leadership didn't sit well with a few. Ex-English Heritage (the body which looks after the welfare of many famous historical sites), Michael's passion for archaeology and the symbolism and knowledge of prehistoric cultures gave him an intense interest in the appearance of crop glyphs, which seemed to him to embody the same ancient wisdom.

Believing implicitly that many of the crop formations were not man-made, Michael was well aware that what the CCCS lacked in credibility was that despite a wealth of unexplained events, effects and statistics, no *absolutely provable* evidence existed to show the world that here was something beyond the work of pranksters. Doug and Dave, the pensioners who had recently claimed they had made all the crop patterns, however discredited they may have been to anyone with an inside knowledge of just how complex and widespread the circles phenomenon really was, had convinced many that it was not to be taken seriously. Although the circles had returned to the fields of England once more in 1992, something was needed to put them firmly back on the map of the unexplained. One of the things which could achieve this, Michael believed, was a film or video showing a formation being created by unknown forces...

Such a video would turn scientific opinion about the circles on its head. Those who had so far scoffed would be forced to admit that the crop formations could not all be the work of jokers. A few would accuse the video of being fake but those with any sense would at last realise that here was a truly 'paranormal' phenomenon. Wouldn't they..?

The Ones That Got Away...

Despite several attempts to obtain a video of a glyph forming, no research group had yet been successful. The investigators Colin Andrews and Pat Delgado had tried two years running to gain the elusive visual evidence by covering circle-prone areas with sophisticated cameras and equipment in the hope that a pattern might form within their range. In 1989, *Operation White Crow* at Cheesefoot Head just outside Winchester had produced a number of anomalous events but no video. The follow-up venture *Operation Blackbird* in 1990 turned into a media circus debacle, when, after much excited rhetoric broadcast on national television, lights filmed in the sky turned out to be a hot air balloon and a formation which appeared the same night was discovered to be an obvious hoax. With a crucifix and *Horoscope* board game placed carefully inside, the circles had been deliberately perpetrated by persons unknown to make the researchers - and thus the phenomenon - look silly. When what was believed to be a genuine glyph *did* actually appear in front of the *Blackbird* cameras, it was too far away for any real conclusions to be drawn from the very fuzzy images, although rumour persists to this day that real and clear footage *was* taken but kept secret. Unviewed secret films are no good to anyone, however.

In 1991, a similar operation, *Project Chameleon*, had also drawn a blank, albeit in spectacular style. With sophisticated motion detectors placed around an area of fields and with infra-red night-sight cameras trained, researchers settled down one evening to see if the circle-making forces would grace them with their presence. A heavy mist came down and the night passed uneventfully. When morning came and the grey lifted, there were two crop formations right next to the surveillance caravans, one which suggested the shape of a question mark... Nothing had been videoed, no motion detected. Everything about the mischievous behaviour of whatever was creating the circles seemed to suggest that it wasn't ready to be caught in the act.

Eye-Witness Accounts

And yet, there had been eye-witnesses to the creation of crop patterns. Most famously, a couple from Surrey, Vivien and Gary Tomlinson, claimed to have had a circle form around their feet. Their story has been treated with scepticism by those who don't wish the phenomenon to be anything out of the ordinary and they have been misquoted and misrepresented on several occasions. At the end of 1994, Barry Reynolds and I interviewed the Tomlinsons to get to the bottom of the story. We were happy that they were telling the truth as they knew it.

Their version of events ran like this: One warm evening in 1989, as they walked along a footpath which crossed a local field, the Tomlinsons observed a strange "band of mist" pass quickly across the field. Although the evening was humid and still, nearby trees started to sway as if struck by a sudden wind. A kind of whirlwind "just seemed to appear from nowhere... it seemed to literally drop from the sky". The vortex was "shimmering" with electrical-type activity and giving off a high-pitched "pan-pipe-like" sound according to Vivien; "There were various notes, it wasn't just one, and then at one point there was just one continuous really high note... My ears went funny at that stage. I felt pain in my ears." The whirlwind struck them: "We were being buffeted. I saw Gary's hair standing on end and I could feel my whole body tingling. Gary says the same, and he saw my hair standing up, and we were pulled off the path."

As Vivien and Gary were forced by the buffeting into the standing crop, the stems began to spiral downward around them, laid by lots of little mini-whirlwinds "running around on the side", all glowing, "wrapping 'round the corn and bringing it down" at "an incredible speed". The main vortex which seemed to contain the other little ones suddenly broke in two; "The second seemed to be like a pillar going all the way up into the sky, just like a tube". This moved off across the field leaving a zigzag trail in the crop before forming another circle nearby. The anticlockwise circle the Tomlinsons were left standing in was only a few feet across, with a small upright tuft left between the two of them. As the strange whirlwinds moved away and out of sight, Gary and Vivien stumbled out of the field in shock, feeling nauseous and totally bemused by the experience they had just had. Vivien was later to discover that her eardrums had been perforated by the experience. Neither of them were aware of the crop circle phenomenon at this time and it wasn't until the pictogram formations hit the headlines the following year that they realised exactly what it was they had witnessed and came forward with their story.

Other stories of people watching circles forming in a matter of seconds have been recorded, notably the experience of Martin Sohn-Rethel in Kingston, near Lewes, East Sussex, recorded in *Fields of Mystery*. If it was possible to *watch* this process taking place, surely it was possible to video it? But one would have to be in absolutely the right place at the right time. Was it coincidence that all of the people who reported seeing formations being created were not enthusiasts and didn't know much beforehand about what they had witnessed? The circle-making forces, ever wily and seemingly with purpose, appeared keen to prevent those who might actually *want* a film of such an event happening from having it. There seemed little point in expending too much energy and finance covering fields with cameras in blind hope. Another approach was clearly needed. The phenomenon had shown on many occasions that it seemed to know what was being said and thought about it. If researchers wanted to video a circle forming, perhaps they had to *ask*. With this idea in mind, Michael Green came across the Joeb communications.

Formation with a standing centre probably not unlike that which Vivien and Gary Tomlinson described forming around them. This particular circle was part of what became known as the 'DNA' formation, a chain of spiralling circles at Alton Barnes, Wiltshire, 1996.

The Project Initiated

Michael had long been a student of psychic communications and had a discerning eye for what he considered genuine mediums and the integrity of their channelled entities. He was immediately impressed by the Joeb transcriptions and was even more encouraged that they came from a member of CCCS Sussex. Ever on the lookout for reliable field researchers, Michael had shown open admiration for the efficiency and enthusiasm of the Sussex team, who had successfully documented all the regional 1992 formations. With such a combination of a pure psychic contact and a group of dependable young enthusiasts (as the heart of the Sussex crew largely were), Michael saw an opportunity to put into action a plan he had been formulating for some time - to arrange, via a psychic medium to transmit messages directly to their source, a rendezvous point with the circle-making forces, whereby, with their agreement, they would create a crop pattern in front of video cameras. His intentions were outlined neatly in a paper he circulated to chosen individuals entitled *Communication With The Crop Circle Makers*.

Michael contacted the Sussex group early in 1993 to put forward the idea, and had a series of meetings with Paul and Joeb, where he became convinced they were the right channels to act as go-betweens from this world to the realms of the circle-making forces, which he believed, as did Joeb, were largely Devic in origin. Joeb made clear that he was not a circle-maker himself nor was in direct contact with them, however, his "mistress" the Earth Mother was and he agreed to act as a link - but with no guarantees. Paul describes Joeb's connection with the circles' source:

"Shortly after that initialising rain-lashed night when Joeb first made contact he said: *"You called on my lady, the Earth Goddess, whom I love and adore. I am her servant. You called her and got me!"* Joeb spoke often of his love for 'My Lady' as he so often referred to her. Soon he was to call her 'Ayesha', the name she was revered as during one of his lives as a young Priest at a stone circle near what is now Sudbury, Suffolk."

Michael was impressed by this. Writing in Paul's book *Joeb: Servant of Gaia*, he said:

"The tribal people Joeb describes worshipped the Earth Goddess as 'Ayesha'. No such

One day in 1993, a group of us set out to find the site of a long-vanished stone circle which Joeb had described at what is now Sudbury, Suffolk, home to one of his previous lives. David Russell and Quenton survey the discovered area, found exactly as we had been told.

Goddess was known amongst the Celtic peoples, but in Northern Europe at this time the collective name for deity was 'Aesir', a specialist detail of which Paul is most unlikely to have been aware."

Devas

Joeb began to tell us more about the Devas, as Paul recalls:

"Joeb often spoke about Devic forces (intelligent beings that are associated with Earth, Air, Fire, Water, Animal, Vegetable and Mineral: the seven kingdoms of nature) and referred to these forces as: "*My little friends of whom I'm well aware.*" The Earth Mother herself is a Devic being and all Devic forces come under her command. In fact it is she who creates them as they are an extension of herself. These little beings are an expression of Ayesha but also have their own life and work. The Earth Goddess acknowledges a force outside of herself. She, like us, is slowly clawing her way back to the infinite Source, 'The One', or 'God'. Except that she is not shackled to religion or man-made belief systems. Joeb was NOT a Devic Being, he made that very clear, but he understood them, as I was beginning to."

Joeb described the Devas thus:

"The Devic forces are points of energy, some people call them fairies. And these forces, these energy fields, help to create the etheric counterpart of a tree, say. And upon this etheric counterpart is built the physical. These energy fields, these points of light, these intelligences, are all under one Deva. You have a tree Deva, a flower Deva and so on. These are streams of consciousness which all come under the Earth Mother."

However, the Devas were not just unthinking binding forces but could split themselves into separate intelligent beings linked by a group consciousness, maintaining and protecting the planet. Paul elaborates:

"Devas, or nature spirits, are as free as the wind itself (expressions of the Earth Mother, a little Tree Elf friend once told me: "*The Earth Mother created us*"). They answer to nobody but the Earth Mother and themselves, leaving aside the angelic being referred to in mythology as archangel Michael. He is their guardian! As depicted in countless children's story books the Devas are mischievous and cheeky, love to joke and prank. They also love music and dance and bask in the joys of nature, of which they are a part. They can also be called the 'mechanics' of the planet. Joeb's information from Ayesha was that the creation of a crop circle was largely Devic, though not totally, and without the help and co-operation of these forces they would not, could not, appear. Although the circles were created to open the minds of humankind they were also expressions of the Goddess herself, trying to explain how uncomfortable she was now, how she had to change. The pain was caused by humankind in their abuse of her body as if she were nothing but a lump of rock floating in space instead of the vibrant, living being that she was, a being that fed, clothed and sheltered us. Yet when she complained of her ill-treatment, nobody wanted to listen."

"Joeb's description of Ayesha was of a living energy-mass, pulsating with colour and sound. Many of these colours were of a frequency in a spectrum that we, in our three-dimensional tunnel vision, have no concept of. He saw her expression through every leaf, every tree, every ocean, every rain-puddle, worshipped her and became a worker, a representative, a devotee. His job was to tell us of her beauty and destiny, a destiny closely linked to that of we human beings clinging so tightly to three-dimensional reality. He was here to help us loosen our grip without falling."

Just one of the many stunning crop formations which have appeared over the years. This seems to have a scorpion-like quality to it. Bishops Cannings, Wiltshire, 1994. Photo: Steve Alexander

This crop design appears to show a chart of the inner part of the Earth's solar system, presumably as seen from our vantage point - which is perhaps why the Earth itself isn't marked. Longwood Warren, Hampshire, 1995. Photo: Steve Alexander

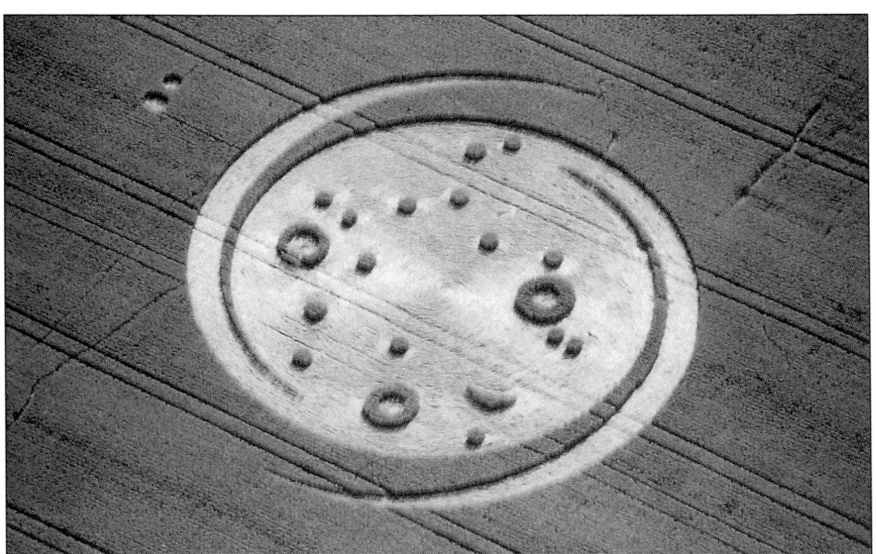

Above: One of several astonishing 'galaxy' formations in the same year. West Stowell, Wiltshire, 1994. Photo: Steve Alexander

Right: Stonehenge has been at the centre of crop formation activity in the 'Wessex' area, as can be seen from the proximity of this huge design in 1996. Photo: Steve Alexander

In a paper entitled *A Challenge From The Crop Circle Makers*, circulated amongst key members of the Centre for Crop Circle Studies, Michael Green summed up Joeb's description of the circle-making process:

"*1) The basic motive behind the creation of this phenomenon is to awaken the 'Seed People' amongst humanity to their responsibility at this time by the use of symbols acting on their subconscious.*

2) Although extra-terrestrial intelligences are involved (the 'Space People'), the initiative, formulation and creation of the crop circle phenomenon is wholly under the direction of our own Global Intelligence. This being, who is described as Gaia or the Earth Mother is known in the Timeless Wisdom as the Earth Logos. 'She' is working through the intelligences of the natural world who are generally termed Devas.

3) The 'beings' responsible for the crop formations are living intelligences working under God (however defined), who deserve the same consideration and courtesy that we should extend to members of the human family. The real challenge of these communications is that if we, as investigators of this phenomenon, wish to communicate and work with these other beings it will require a drastic and far-reaching change in our attitude and behaviour; we must accept that they exist and be prepared to joyfully work in love and harmony with them and each other."

The core members of CCCS Sussex shared Michael and Paul's enthusiasm for the communication project, honoured to have been chosen for the task, well aware that some other CCCS groups around the country might make similar attempts, although only Sussex seemed to have a working psychic among them. Given the previous failure of others to video formations being created there certainly seemed little point in spending cold, dark hours outside in the vain hope that something might happen. To actually *arrange* an occurrence seemed much more positive. Few in the team had been exposed to psychic work before and perhaps because of this all who were made privy to the project shared a kind of childlike, uncynical enthusiasm for it, willing to give anything a go.

The Team

Controversially, to ensure the integrity of the experiment, it was decided not to involve the whole branch of CCCS Sussex and to restrict knowledge of the work to those who would share enthusiasm for the type of methods to be used. This ruled out certain key members who could certainly be relied on but who didn't believe psychic communication was a viable way to conduct research. If we were to gain the piece of video footage we were aiming for, maintaining integrity was paramount to ensure that no individual would misuse the results or jeopardise the project by telling others of what was occurring, thus laying it open to accusations that the team could have been duped by outside *provocateurs*. Even so, it would take a while to get the mix just right, as we would discover.

In addition to Paul, Michael and myself, two others were closely involved with what would become an ongoing activity for the next three summers.

Barry Reynolds had documented many of the Sussex crop circles in 1990 and 1991 and played a key role in gathering together the people who made up CCCS Sussex. Tall and dashing in a sort of *Boys Own*-style, Barry was an adventurer by night (a Venture Scout leader) and a logical realist by day (a computer consultant), not given to flights of fancy that fell outside of the scientific method. Despite his straight approach to the crop circle phenomenon, something attracted Barry to the idea of using psychic guidance to achieve an end and his attitudes would mellow over the next few years leaving him more open-minded to the concept of spiritual dimensions.

Martin Noakes was another straight-thinker whose views would be remoulded as time went by. A musician by profession (the only member of the team to have the accolade of having once appeared on *Top of the Pops*, with the band *Red Box*), Martin was a firm nuts-and-bolts UFO believer when asked what created crop circles, but again, was willing to give the idea a go that the circle-making forces could be contacted or influenced by psychic means.

Together, all at this point in our late twenties, early thirties, the three of us made up a trinity of what Barry called 'the naughty boys'; we continually joked and made light of the incredible events which were coming into our lives. It was simply our way and didn't mean that we didn't take seriously the work we were doing in the fields and beyond. Humour was, as Joeb often said, a positive energy raiser in any case. Some new to the group would sometimes find this hard to deal with and Michael Green seemed at first a little taken aback by our approach but, given our good results, grew to tolerate it!

As we began to realise the gravity of what would happen if our experiment was successful, Barry in particular felt that the more who could witness the event, the better, and thus a number of other people, by invitation and mutual agreement with the existing team, came on board. We would realise later the difficulty of trying to co-ordinate such a large group of people to share one aim. Through Mark and Jason Porthouse (who at this point were not deeply involved with CCCS Sussex or the project) two further psychics became involved, Carole Coren and Diana Summer, both of whom had been receiving similar channelled communications to the Joeb messages. Diana channelled vocally, like Paul, and Carole received her messages through 'automatic writing' where her thoughts would be guided by an outside influence while she held a pen or sat at a computer. Carole's then boyfriend, Adam Cotton, an amateur pilot who would later fly some of us over the Sussex formations in 1993, had also asked to be part of the project. John Cole, who had introduced Paul to CCCS Sussex, was along for the ride, together with Paul's teenage nephew Quenton Cole (no relation to John). Lastly, Ted Richards, a scientist whose main interest was UFOs and who had conducted a number of scientific experiments for the main CCCS, was invited to join in. All were under strict instructions not to tell anyone of their involvement .

The team was complete. Now we had to discover exactly what we would have to do to bring about the much hoped for rendezvous with the circle-making forces.

A Time And A Place

Clearly, for any rendezvous to take place, a time and a place had to be fixed. Early conversations with Joeb, who, as far as the team could tell, was transmitting our requirements back to the circle-making forces through his channels, had suggested that we would simply be told through him where and when we should gather for the experiment. In fact, things happened rather differently. One April night, Paul was given a vision:

"Visions and information do not always conform to one's will, that is, the information required seems to have a life out-of-time. It very often comes when IT wants to and, in my case, very often when I am trying to sleep. Of course this is a very receptive time and makes a certain amount of sense. Yet when one sits down and purposefully opens up one's clairvoyant screen, after making a request for certain facts, it doesn't always come. One's mental and physical state has a lot to do with it and like any gift you need to keep it in good shape and PRACTICE."

"I had already asked Joeb to show me a site for our experiment. It had to have the element of water and the presence of an earth energy line. At first nothing of any significance came into view and, like most things, one can try too hard. So I let go and waited for the information, if any, to come my way. It was a couple of nights later when sleep evaded me. I tried every mental trick I knew in order to 'get off'. Nothing worked. I then began to realise that I had to open my screen and tune-in to my psychic self. I lay on my back and waited. I didn't have to wait long: the vision of a huge devil standing astride a ditch made itself known. I knew that this was symbolic and nothing to be afraid of. My devil wore a large belt and its buckle was made out of the letters J. U. N. E. In each of his hands he held a number. As he faced me, his right hand held the number two and his left hand held the number seven. It was pretty obvious what was being said here. The location was Devil's Dyke, a huge rift-valley which had been used as an Iron Age hill-fort, just outside of Brighton. The month and the date: the 27th June. But whereabouts at Devil's Dyke?"

Ever keen to double-check his results with others, Paul felt he needed to meet with the other two channellers Diana and Carole to determine the vision's accuracy and to gain a clearer picture of where exactly at Devil's Dyke the group would need to wait for the monumental event. Whether we ourselves were choosing the dates and locations through self-divination and the circle-making forces were simply intending to attend accordingly, or whether the visions were being 'transmitted' from elsewhere to cue us to the conclusions arrived at was unclear. Whatever the case, the meeting of the three psychics, who conducted a 'remote viewing' in which real places are visualised from a distance, produced results which seemed so definite that there was little doubt that these were the directions that should be followed. Joeb would later confirm them. Paul describes the gathering and the remarkable visions which resulted:

"I had known Carole for a few months now and knew that as an 'automatic writer' she was pretty good; she had been receiving messages from her guide 'Shomas'. I had not, however, met her friend Diana, who I understood was also a damn good psychic. I phoned Carole and asked whether she and Diana would care to have a meeting with me to see whether we could get a location through visionary means for our proposed crop circle experiment. I also needed to double-check my Devil's Dyke clairvoyance. Both agreed to meet at my place in the house of saucers."

"Carole sat with her pad on her lap, pen poised. Diana and I sat and studied our 'inner screens'. Almost immediately my 'devil' appeared exactly as before. I mentioned this. Diana started to see a pool of water with trees growing around it, some of their roots actually in the water. Carole described a similar scene saying that it opened onto a sloping piece of land which, in her mind, she soared down as if on a big dipper. She also saw a fox! Diana went on with more detail: she visualised a fence at the back of the pool. By now my devil had disappeared and been replaced with the pool. I saw that a track ran beside the fence and that an earth energy line ran straight through the water, down the slope and into a field of crop."

"That was the best that we could do and we all felt pretty pleased. But all this had to be proved. We now had to find this pool and its fence, track and energy line... and what of the fox? I had to do some serious dowsing, and soon!"

Paul sketched a crude map from what had been learned. Then, using a pendulum and a 1:50000 Ordnance Survey map, he dowsed the general area of Devil's Dyke to pinpoint exactly the site witnessed in the meditation:

"In dowsing, especially if the information is vital, one has to keep a very firm check on one's emotions. Most dowsers rarely ask for personal information concerning their intimate, private life, or indeed a project that is very special and pertinent to them simply because emotion and the 'I want THIS to be the answer' syndrome can get in the way of the truth. It is at this time that we call in an independent 'checker', someone not emotionally involved with the project, whatever it might be."

A puzzle to Paul was that the location he and his 'checkers' finally came up with at nearby Saddlescombe didn't show a pool, which had been so strong in the vision. When Barry then produced a 1:25000 map, which showed finer detail, Paul was delighted to find that there was indeed not one but two ponds marked on the map, displaying a layout uncannily similar to his initial sketch. Now there was nothing for it but to head out for the location in reality.

The pond, visualised by the three psychics and subsequently discovered at Saddlescombe, site of the first rendezvous experiment.

Visions Fulfilled

With anticipation and a little apprehension, one Sunday afternoon in early May 1993, Barry, Martin, Paul, Quenton and myself, together with assorted family members out for the ride, set out for the Saddlescombe side of the Devil's Dyke area. The Dyke itself was half a mile or so north-west from the spot which dowsing had selected.

Paul waited in his car, tucked into the small farm track which would provide such a useful parking space in the next few weeks, waiting for the scouting party to report back:

"I watched as Andy, Barry, Quenton and the others took the upward climb through a sun-kissed day toward a small group of trees that, until then, existed only as a mark on an Ordnance Survey map. I 'knew' they were heading for the destined point but my in-built 'doubt' ability was also in full flood. I was a mess!"

"As the figures receded and the crick in my neck tightened I resorted to psychic means. I closed my eyes. Momentarily, a picture of the pool of water, the trees and the little fence hovered in my mind. I felt Joeb's presence, his excitement. *"They're going to find it, Paul, they're going to find it."*

A public footpath ran up onto open downland, which bordered a crop field to the east below. At the top of the hill, we were astounded to find everything the three psychics had predicted. There was the pond with trees around it, their roots dangling down into the water - the second one on the map had long since dried up. Behind this ran a fence and from the pond, going eastwards, was a sloping field of grass and scrubland where cattle grazed (Carole's 'big dipper' ride). All these had been positively visualised by our remote viewers and if there was any doubt left amongst the non-psychics that here was an experiment worth taking part in, it dissolved at this point. Across the country road which passed through the valley were yet more fields, no houses within sight. Up here, on open ground, we wouldn't be disturbed as we held our vigil. All was perfect. We were on to something - we had found our spot.

The view from where we would sit at Saddlescombe, showing the grassland sloping down to the field below.

But then a moment of confusion struck - if we were to video a crop circle being formed, surely there had to be some crop for the circle-making forces to perform in? Up here, despite everything being perfectly anticipated, there was no cultivated field, only long grass. Gradually it dawned: at the foot of the sloping downland from the pond was a narrow strip of barley, the stems still young and green. Paul had forgotten to tell us that in the vision this was where we were to look. To video a pattern being formed, we would need to look *down* on it. Film of vague movements in a flat field would help convince no-one. This spot was clearly where we were meant to *stand* and set up our cameras, not, as some of us had assumed, where the formation would appear. From the top of the slope we had an ideal view of the field below us which by June would be turning ripe and golden. Facing east, we would be able to video our gift being created with enough elevation to capture it on camera with ease.

Quenton dowsed for the energy line. Sure enough, it ran from the pond to the field below, as Paul had seen. It was time to return with the good news to our man in the car. All this time, Paul was sitting, anxiously awaiting word from the top of the hill:

"I waited. After a while I felt a huge surge of excitement. They had found something, they had found the pool!"

"I watched as they made their slow pace down the hill, watched as they disappeared momentarily in a dip of trees, watched as their faces gradually took familiar form making their way towards me, scanned their body language intently as they climbed the gate only a few yards in front of my car. There was no sign of emotion, no excitement, nothing. My stomach contracted into a tight ball. It had been a failure. But what was this? Smiles, outstretched hands to shake mine? Hugs? Andy said: "We found it. It was exactly as you and the girls had said and in exactly the spot you dowsed." I was suddenly a very happy medium."

The date and location for our rendezvous had been found. Of that we were in no doubt. Now all that remained was to gather the members of the group together into a coherent team and to prepare ourselves for the big event...

The field (here seen in winter) where we hoped our crop formation was going to appear...

View from the lower slopes of Wolstonbury Hill; from here Barry watched the movements of a glowing ball of light. The luminosity came from the general direction of the two houses, across the field towards the centre of the picture, before crossing the dual carriageway and disappearing into the trees.

3: SIGNS AND PORTENTS

'One Mind'

During the run up to the date of our first experiment, Michael, Barry and myself regularly liaised with Paul and Joeb to discuss the details of what was expected of us to ensure a successful result. We were assured that the Devic realms were willing to co-operate as long as certain conditions were met. The overriding point made was that the Devas were distrustful of humankind and that to win their faith everyone in the team had to be of '*one mind*' and be involved for the right reasons. Any hint of doubt, negativity or intent to misuse the situation for personal gain might scare the circle-making forces away. Joeb explained the Devic point of view:

"You are viewed as walking circuit boards - that is the way it is - walking energy fields. They view you and they see the mud and the sludge that is inside the auric fields. They see you as beings of light ...and when they sense harmony in your aura they are attracted to you. ...They like to see a circuit board that does not have a blockage. ...You must learn to radiate love and positivity as that is what they wish to see. If you have this, they will do their work."

It had already been agreed that should the experiment be a success the footage would belong to the group as a whole, regardless of whose camera captured the scene. The arrival of such proof in amongst the crop circle community would be a huge responsibility to place on the shoulders of one and the huge attention and pressure could give rise to temptations to use the sequence for personal fame and fortune. To protect the integrity of the project, shared copyright ownership was decided in advance. For such an understanding to hold good, it was therefore vital that the team was indeed of 'one mind'.

And yet, even as late as May, the entire company of eleven had never met together. All the decisions and arrangements had been made by telephone and only the core of Paul, Michael, Barry, Martin and myself had kept up regular contact. It was time to rectify this and a meeting of everyone involved was called for May 25th at the Scout Centre in Burgess Hill.

Cracks Appear

It was immediately apparent from the poor turnout of only five of the expected eleven people on May 25th that certain participants weren't taking the project as seriously as others. Despite the stressed importance of attending the get-together to discuss the fine detail of the rendezvous now only a month away, some made excuses and others simply didn't appear. Worried by this alarming sign of incohesion, the five of us who made it adjourned to the *Potters Arms* across the road for a more informal briefing than had been planned.

Worse still, it became clear that some individuals were not happy with the inclusion of certain others in the project, suspicious of their motives or simply because they didn't know them. There were even (unfounded as it turned out) rumours that some had invited all their friends to come along and that secrecy had been broken. It was felt, rather elitistly and unfairly in retrospect, that maybe some would not be capable of comprehending the staggering spectacle we were hoping would unfold before us. But by now it was too late to tell people that they couldn't take part. The decision by the core team to invite others on board had been taken for practical reasons which seemed to make sense at the time and there was no going back now. However, this fragmentation did not deem well for an experiment which had to be free from all negativity.

Good Omens

Despite concerns about the team's unity, an astonishing event then occurred which greatly encouraged us that perhaps, after all, we were on the right track.

The most major meeting yet with Joeb to finalise arrangements for the 27th had

The 'triangular triplet' design found as close to Paul's house as a formation could get on the morning of a major rendezvous meeting. Note the proximity of the houses, yet no-one saw or heard anything.

been called at Paul's house for 6th June. At 8.30am that morning, Barry received a telephone call to inform him that the very first Sussex crop formation of 1993 had been discovered; a 'triangular triplet' - one circle surrounded by three satellites. It was found in very young green wheat next to a housing estate at Sompting. The field had no tractor 'tramlines' and the crop had seemingly been only lightly brushed by whatever force laid it down. But most importantly, it was in the closest field to Paul's house at nearby Lancing as one could get...

This was an extremely good omen, almost as if the circle-making forces were giving us a sign of encouragement, granting their blessing to the meeting taking place there that day, and thus hopefully to the experiment itself. Despite all the assurances from Joeb and channelled sources, we mere mortals still needed some kind of concrete evidence that we were indeed interacting with them. This appeared to be it.

The farmer was contacted and arrangements were hastily made to get down to the formation before the meeting, to be held early that afternoon. When Barry, Martin and myself arrived at the site we were astounded to see its configuration. In addition to the plans for the rendezvous team, CCCS Sussex had as a whole carried out meditations at the previous two branch meetings, concentrating on a particular pattern to see if the appearance of a crop glyph's shape could be influenced by the power of thought (we would bring this idea to the fore in a much bigger way in 1995).

The symbol we had chosen to contemplate was three circles in a triangle, joined by

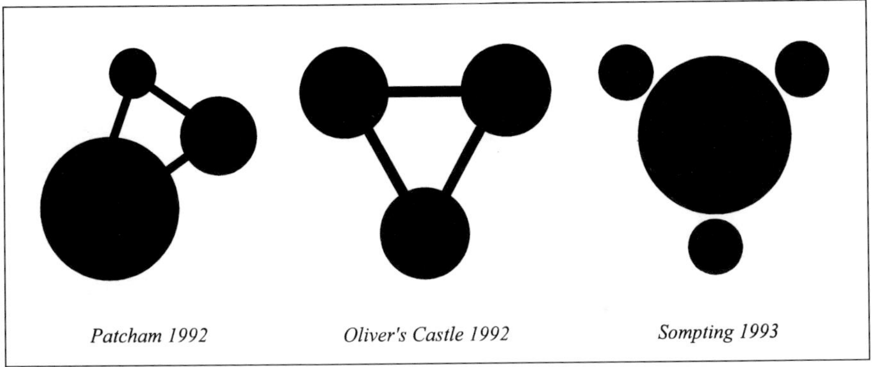

The three crop symbols linked by the CCCS Sussex meditation experiments.

pathways. Incredibly, none of us were aware then that a) this was the logo of CSETI, an American project which had been attempting to contact extra-terrestrials through similar meditational and other methods, or that b) this symbol had appeared in a field at Olivers Castle, near Devizes in Wiltshire, in response to another thought experiment by a group of CSETI members in 1992. We were aware of the shape's similarities to a crop formation which had appeared at Patcham, East Sussex in 1992, but that was all.

The triangular triplet which arrived at Sompting was not exactly the pattern the branch members had concentrated on but certainly seemed to be a mutated version of it. Another good omen!

The three of us spent the morning examining the pattern from the top floor of a house belonging to the lady who had reported the event, and vowed to return later. When Michael arrived at lunchtime and heard about the formation, he was eager to see this sign from the circle-making forces for himself. After our fruitful meeting with Joeb was concluded and fine details for the 27th had been discussed, we set out for the field once again, in blinding hot sunshine, Michael in tow.

Neighbours must have been rather curious to have seen four men, led by the tall figure of Michael, decked out in resplendent white that day, crowded into a lady's

A closer look at our uncannily well-timed visitor. The crop was so young it sprang up again almost immediately, making the circles of the triangular triplet very faint.

bedroom, leaning dangerously out of the window which overlooked the field... Local elderly residents in sheltered accommodation were even more surprised when Michael heard that one of their gentlemen had spent the night sitting by an open window that night, and decided to pay him a visit to see if he had witnessed anything strange. One apartment was thus treated to the delightfully surreal experience of having an entire crop circle investigation team trudge into its living room, cameras, rucksacks and notepads at the ready, led by a tall authoritative figure in a wide-brimmed hat. Small white-haired ladies sat primly against the wall, in wide-eyed awe at this 'official visit' from (what we later heard ourselves somewhat misleadingly described as) "important scientists". Extending his hand to all, Michael announced himself with pride: "Good afternoon. My name is Michael Green and I'm the Chairman of the Centre for Crop Circle Studies..." We all nodded courteously. It was probably their most exciting day for a long time.

The Appliance Of Science?

Spirit revitalised by the visitation of the triangular triplet, it was decided to attempt another gathering of all involved in the experiment. Held once again at Burgess Hill, this time there was a much better turnout.

Ted, a scientist ever-keen to try out new gadgets and techniques to catch the circle-making forces in the act, was concerned by some of the conditions which the Devic forces had apparently laid down via Joeb. Paul reiterated at the meeting that only video cameras would be allowed on site, no other electrical equipment. We were told that the Devas operated on a frequency of existence which could be disrupted by electrical activity. For the rendezvous to work, they could allow for a number of camcorders at a distance, but anything else might be a risk to them. Ted was unhappy with this. He wanted to lace the field with gadgets to test and measure the forces that might be applied when the crop formation was created. To appease his concerns, Paul agreed to a smaller meeting with Ted whereby these issues could be aired.

With only a week to go before the 27th June, Ted spoke with Joeb at Paul's house. He was met with the same resistance though; only video cameras, nothing else, would be allowed. Piqued at the refusal to budge, Ted protested that his equipment would not be giving off any discernible interference or unnatural waves, but he was firmly, though politely, rebuffed. At this, Ted's enthusiasm for the project, understandably, began to wane but he still agreed to take part.

Paul Becomes A Field

In the days running up to the long-awaited rendezvous, Paul had a profound experience which would connect him more firmly to the canvas we were hoping our crop formation would appear in and which he would never forget:

"During all the mayhem and bluster in our quest to connect with something outside of ourselves I wondered long and hard about the plants that we were trampling, analysing, dissecting and, indeed, eating! The living corn of this planet that for us would be the focus of so much hope and glory, despair and gloom. What, if anything, did the corn itself think about all this?"

"As a medium I'd entered many streams of consciousness (with some success); Devic forces, beings from other planets and discarnate humans. Once I even entered the spirit

All living things have consciousness - even fields of wheat (here seen at Sompting), as Paul was to discover!

of a tree (resulting in the story *The Oak on the Plain*, see appendices) an experience that had a profound and lasting effect on me."

"So why not try and enter the mass consciousness of a field of corn, like that we would be working with on the 27th? It couldn't be any more barmy then anything else I'd done. I lay on my bed and went into channelling mode, making the request that I 'become' a field of corn!"

"After a few minutes I felt my body begin to undulate like a flag flying gently in the breeze. My vision spread out beyond the confines of my small bedroom. I felt and 'saw' that my room was now a field of waving crops that stretched away into the distance. As the wind blew and the rain buffeted me I was in ecstasy. I knew that the nodes of every stalk of corn were stimulated by the wind and rain. They welcomed the elements as old friends. And as the nodes were stimulated so then were the roots galvanised into action to draw up water and nourishment. The nodes were all-important, a little like the brain in humankind. This ecstatic feeling was almost sexual, wonderful beyond words. There was no effort here, no yearning for something better. I/the corn field were who we were. That was all. I became aware of other fields of cereal and realised I could communicate with them. It was so delightful that I didn't really want it to end."

"If I ever have to come back to Earth again then let me choose to be a field of corn, I would not complain. We so underestimate the world, the reality around us. Just stopping to smell the flowers now and again suddenly becomes not enough. In this physical school of so-called reality perhaps we should all try harder."

Sweet Dreams?

The uncanny discovery of the triangular triplet was the first in a series of strange events which would happen to the group or individuals connected with it as the project progressed. These experiences seemed to suggest that the very act of making overtures of communication to other realms somehow opened the participants up to bizarre occurrences which might otherwise never have happened, unless they were extremely odd coincidences. It was as if, by attempting to tune in to other frequencies, we were opening gateways to other energies and levels of awareness. I was to have such an experience, if a disconcerting one, shortly before 27th June.

One evening I was listening to a song about the deconstruction of the Berlin Wall. Later, as my wife Kaye and I slept in the darkness of the early hours, I found myself dreaming about the famous television sequences of the wall being attacked by eager Germans with power tools. Suddenly these vivid images were shattered by an incredibly loud grinding noise which snapped both of us awake, our hearts pounding. This wasn't just in my mind; Kaye was alert too. We were both scared. The room was filled with a near-deafening buzzing. Its source seemed to be directly above our heads. I reached up to touch the wall - it was vibrating violently. I instinctively knew that this sound was a projection of my dream, as if the machines eating into the concrete of the Berlin Wall were attempting to break into reality. If not, why would our adjoining neighbours be drilling into the partition at three in the morning? Abruptly, the noise ceased. Shaken and confused, we settled back to sleep. An hour later we were brutally awoken again by the same intrusion. We pulled the duvet over our heads in an effort to blot it out.

Next day we spoke to our neighbours. They had heard nothing. Paul and Diana believed that my psychic 'shell' had cracked and that all this exposure to clairvoyant activity was having more than a passive effect. But instead of receiving, I was unwittingly transmitting! Diana gave me a wooden talisman of protection, and although I was never to become a psychic as such, I had to learn to contain my dreams rather better in the future.

Barry Sees The Light

On Sunday 20th June, Barry was leading a team of Venture Scouts in clearing ragwort from grazing land on the lower slopes of Wolstonbury Hill at Pyecombe, West Sussex, not far from the site of two crop formations in 1990 and 1991. At 1.00pm, the Venture Unit broke for lunch and, with the exception of Barry and his two young sons, headed back to their cars to eat. Barry remained on the side of the hill, facing west, looking down on the A23 dual carriageway from Brighton to London.

At about 1.15pm, in strong sunshine, Barry looked up and suddenly noticed a small luminosity over fields on the opposite side of the A23. He quickly realised it was moving in an almost direct line towards them, from the general area of Devil's Dyke, a mile or so away. As it got closer, it became apparent that this was not a strange reflection, balloon or a bird, but a brightly glowing ball of light.

Commanding his children to stay put, Barry began to stride down the steep hill in an effort to meet the light if it crossed the carriageway. The object appeared to be moving at "running pace", meandering gently from side to side as it moved in an otherwise straight line, and Barry was soon running himself as he realised how fast he would have to go to get to it.

Reaching the edge of the field which bordered the main road, the light grazed the top of the fence and skipped over, straight across the path of the busy A23... As it did so, a pale green saloon car in the left northbound lane screeched to a halt to avoid colliding with it. The glowing object passed harmlessly in front, continuing its unfaltering path and narrowly missing several other speeding cars by only a few feet. The air turbulence from the passing vehicles seemed to have no effect whatsoever on the light which crossed over the fence on Barry's side of the road into a field of sheep. The driver of the car which had to stop, clearly shaken, pulled over into an adjacent lay-by and sat there for the next quarter of an hour.

Barry, meanwhile, was hurtling down the side of the hill and found himself behind a copse of trees through which he could glimpse the light passing swiftly between the grazing sheep. They didn't react at all to the object's presence. Losing the ball in amongst the trees Barry finally gave up the chase, not wanting to leave his children alone any longer.

The length of Barry's sighting and the familiar objects it passed gave him the opportunity to study the light quite carefully as he hared down the hill towards it. It was about the "size of a car wheel" and glowed brilliantly, with indistinct fuzzy edges like radiant energy. Watching a cyclist in fluorescent clothing later from the hill made Barry realise just how bright the light (seen in stark sunlight) was. Its clear path on a day with no more than a mild breeze made it hugely unlikely it was simply a reflective object floating on the wind.

These types of lights had been reported, and on some occasions filmed, by many in the past, often connected with crop formations or earth energy lines. Whether they were just random energies produced by natural geophysical causes - 'earth lights' or 'ball lightning' - following the lines, Devic beings (the 'fairy folk' of old) moving purposefully across the landscape, or, as some believed, 'probes' from extra-terrestrial sources, wasn't known. But such lights would be seen again during the course of the rendezvous experiments carried out by the team.

Like the appearance of the triangular triplet, the gift of such a sighting to one of the main organisers of the communication project seemed to bode well for the 27th June, now only a week ahead. But would such strange forces perform at the crucial moment..?

Barry points out to his son Peter the trajectory of the strange light he watched traversing the A23.

Site of our vigil on the 27th June - the pond lay directly behind the trees and an energy line ran down the slope from the centre of the copse.

A misty dawn breaks over the rendezvous team. Left to right: Ted, Paul, Diana, Carole, Adam and Quenton. (Video image)

4: RENDEZVOUS

Terms And Conditions

Come the day of the rendezvous we had clear instructions about what was expected of us and the list of do's and don'ts had grown longer through conversations with Joeb and advice from Michael and his own channelled sources.

We had been instructed to be settled at the site from 2.00am onwards but we made it clear there would be no point in a crop pattern being created until it was light enough for the video cameras to pick it up. This was apparently understood by the circle-making forces, which Joeb assured us were receiving our messages through him. Although nothing had been promised - indeed Joeb had gone out of his way to state that there could be no *absolute* guarantee that the experiment would be successful - there had also been intimations that in addition to a formation appearing, we might also witness unusual light phenomena in the preceding hours as the site was 'prepared'. In view of Barry's recent experience this didn't seem so far-fetched.

In addition to ensuring harmony and complete positivity within the group, we had been instructed to ritually wash ourselves the night before as a mark of respect to the forces we would be dealing with. We had been advised that light-coloured clothing should be worn, dark being associated with negativity through Devic eyes. There was concern about this as nearly everybody's outdoor clothes were dark - in fact, I nearly always wore black anyway! - and it simply wasn't possible to achieve short of donning druidic robes. A compromise of sorts was reached when some wore light hats, scarves or ribbons on top of their many other layers (much needed at night, even in high summer). At least some of the time waiting was to be spent in meditation or respectful contemplation although we had been told we should enjoy ourselves as well and not take things too seriously. Most of all, it was stressed time and again that there must be no negativity or doubt in the minds of the group. Negative 'auric' energies could even rub off from other people in public places, affecting the odds of success, and this was another reason why personal cleansing was specified. Unfortunately, it would be hard for everyone to meet all these criteria come the night, as we would discover. Paul had his own views on some of the lesser conditions set:

"Ritual cleansing is a powerful tool. But it is no more than a process to concentrate the mind, as indeed is all ritual. For instance, a good dowser doesn't really *need* his tools-of-the-trade. If you are sensitive enough all you need are your hands and a positive mind. So it is with clairvoyance in the form of things like 'reading tea-leaves' or 'casting the bones'. These only serve as visualisation aids which the clairvoyant uses as a psychic drawing-board on which pictures appear. Ritual cleansing, therefore, sharpens the mind and brings it into powerful focus."

The Night Arrives

Finally, after all the months of preparation and expectation, the weekend of the experiment was upon us. The various individuals of the team were to make their way to the site separately at the agreed time. However, four of us gathered first at Barry's house in Burgess Hill on the Saturday night of 26th June. Michael had arrived from the train at teatime and Diana and I turned up around 10.00pm with a view to sleeping a few hours on the floor until it was time to set out for Saddlescombe in Barry's car.

Michael's Lights

When I reached the house, Michael wasn't to be seen. He was sitting out in Barry's floodlit ornamental garden meditating by a pond. Michael had identified this spot as the residence of a tree Deva and felt comfortable there. After a while, an aeroplane passing overhead made him raise his eyes to the sky. As he looked, his attention was drawn to another object travelling south-west to north-east, visually about the size of the moon in the sky. It appeared to be a multi-coloured cluster of lights... The hint of a solid ovoid structure contained the many glowing points. Knowing full well that this was no jet, satellite or helicopter, Michael watched "incredulously" as the object silently sailed across. Ten seconds later it entered a bank of cloud and was gone.

Michael re-entered the house from the patio doors looking visibly pale. As I was about to greet him, he calmly stated "I've just seen a UFO". Everyone in the room stopped, ready to laugh. Realising Michael was deadly serious all suddenly rushed for the door but by now whatever he had seen was gone. Michael seemed quite relaxed with this experience and recounted it undramatically. It seemed to be another omen that we were on to something here. This sighting would not be the last over Barry's house.

The Final Hours

Diana and I bedded down in our sleeping bags on the floor while Michael retreated upstairs to sleep, but sleep was something I couldn't manage. The anticipation of what we were about to do was too great. Many of us were so sure that we were about to achieve our aim that there was no expectation in our minds of anything other than success. The signs were good and we were about to be rewarded by the circle-making forces. No question.

A few clock spins later, in the very early hours of 27th June, four of us were driving through the dark on the way to our great adventure, bright and confident. Dressed with as many layers as movement would permit, we were ready to brave the elements and prepare for the arduous task of lifting several rucksacks full of cameras and video equipment, and - most importantly - one disabled psychic. A big problem ahead was transporting Paul up the side of the South Downs. He certainly couldn't walk it and the only option open to us was to physically lift him over a turnstile and carry him up the steep hill. For this we had procured a stretcher from the British Red Cross but none of us realised quite what an effort this would prove.

A few of our good intentions had already fallen by the wayside. Some of us had managed the ritual cleansing the night before but Carole had to attend her son's birthday party, setting out straight from it, and Martin was playing a gig which he couldn't cancel. Carole *did*, however, see a fox cross the road as she drove to the site - which fulfilled the final part of the visions at Paul's house. Martin came down directly from his gig, arriving significantly late at 3.30am.

Those who could get there on time gathered at about 1.00am, cramming their cars somewhat conspicuously into the small farm track which bordered our barley field at the foot of the hill. We could only hope that the police wouldn't drive past and think an illegal 'rave' was being held.

Barry and I decided that one of the priorities was to get Paul to the site first, ready to channel in case any messages needed to come through. With no lights anywhere in sight, this task was made even harder by the almost pitch blackness in which it had to be executed. With SAS-style tactics, we had agreed that the use of torches be kept to a minimum to avoid alerting any passing farmers or anyone else come to that. Although our experiment was being carried out on open land with a footpath running up to it, we still didn't want to draw unnecessary attention to ourselves in case anyone should disrupt the proceedings.

The attempt to get Paul up the hill was pure comedy. Suddenly able-bodied men were in short supply and it was left to Barry and I to get on with it... Barry began by piggy-backing Paul over the turnstile, no mean feat in itself. Once this hilarious manoeuvre was over, we draped him on the stretcher and picked him up, to his jovial taunts, stomping up the slope, almost blind, in fits, stumbles and starts, pausing every few yards to rest our bursting lungs and aching muscles. The weather, mercifully, was perfect and the stars glinted brightly above us. The Devic forces had done their work there at least. The thought of carrying out this experiment in the pouring rain was not a happy one.

Then, as Barry and I were stumbling along, Paul bouncing around between us, we realised he had gone quiet - except his breathing, which had suddenly become heavy and rhythmic. A familiar booming voice exploded from the blackness - *"Ah, My friends! It is I, Joeb!"*.

What to do? Continue our by now erratic weaving up the slope while holding a conversation with an other-dimensional being, or stop to talk? We opted for the latter, put our channelling friend down and listened to what he had to say. Joeb assured us that all was well. The weather conditions were right and the energies felt good. He was concerned that some of us were taking things a little too seriously, despite a certain amount of childish giggling as we had attempted to heave Paul over the fence and up the hill... Relaxed minds, not tense uptight ones, would provide better energies for the rendezvous.

But another problem soon became apparent. By the time assistance arrived and we finally got Paul (and Joeb, who was at least considerably lighter) to the top, several more twenty minute trips down to the cars had to be made to retrieve the rest of the equipment. When these excursions were finally over and the cameras and videos had been set up, trained on the field below, some of us had very little energy left at all, let alone the positive kind. Still, we were firmly ensconced at last. Our time had come. When Martin eventually turned up, the full quota of eleven people sat waiting in front of the large pond and the trees, looking down onto our field beneath the starlight. We were ready.

Our field at dawn, taken as the tension began to mount and our expectations rose. Something could happen at any moment.

The Moments Of Truth

Joeb began by opening with a small invocation and came through from time to time to assure us that all was well.

With our body temperatures lowering by the minute, we sat or stood, huddled into our thick clothing, as the hours went by. To avoid muddying expensive and weighty wheelchairs, Paul, bizarrely, was slouched in an old toddler buggy. All of us were on the lookout for strange lights or unusual aerial phenomena.

Then, only an hour or so in, to great excitement, an extremely bright light passed slowly overhead from west to east in a straight line. It appeared to be at a very high altitude. It was hard to say whether it was a large satellite or something stranger, but it passed over the horizon and we were never to find out for sure. Nevertheless, it heightened our expectations for something more substantial in our wait for the dawn.

As we grew colder, some of the camaraderie which had punctuated our conversation earlier began to subside and a quiet expectation took over. Now and then we would initiate a specific meditation to try and focus our thoughts but we were ready at any minute to flick the video cameras on if things began to happen.

At about 4.00am, a mist began to rise from the fields and the sky grew pale with dawn. This was the time we had been waiting for. Apart from the bright light, we hadn't seen the display of aerial phenomena some of us had hoped for but perhaps that would come with the arrival of the formation.

An hour or so passed, and with it grew a feeling that something was indeed about to happen. Carole became aware of "Misty etherical beings drifting in front of us, moving about". Adam later described seeing a strange glowing object in the sky which kept appearing and disappearing. A number of us rose to our feet and in unspoken agreement turned on the video cameras. There was tension in the air, almost like an electrical current... This was it, no going back. Joeb instructed us to be ready.

Suddenly, at about 5.15am, down below us in our field, Michael, Adam and Diana perceived a ring of faint blue lights materialise a few feet above the surface of the barley. Michael was the first to break this information quietly and calmly, although the remainder of us couldn't see them ourselves. Perhaps such lights are only visible to those attuned to certain frequencies at particular times. But three of our party of eleven saw them and described the same phenomena. With our legs turned to jelly and our hearts thumping, we waited.

And waited. And waited. And then the tension began to drain from the group. The luminosities vanished from the sight of those who had glimpsed them and we somehow knew a vital moment had passed. Sensing success slipping away from us, we quickly agreed to join hands in an attempt to focus energies and confirm our unity. But a brief glimpse around showed clearly that though our hands may have been joined, our thoughts weren't. One member of the group looked bored and disillusioned, another was glancing casually around at the scenery as if in embarrassment. With a ghastly sinking feeling we began to realise we had blown it.

Cereal Killer

At this point, Carole received a psychic message through her writing, scribbled in the notebook which she took with her everywhere. It read:

"*We wait for all to be sure. We wait for all to believe. There is one who doubts amongst you. You must overcome the doubt and negativity they emit by exuding more positive energy yourself. I know you wish this to happen but as time goes on doubt creeps in. Keep positive, keep wanting it to happen. There is still time. We have promised something and we still wish it to happen. Give off positive energy. I know it is not easy waiting but we cannot perform before sceptics.*"

A perfect illustration that the team was not of 'one mind' came in the hour after what might have been the moment of truth. In stunned silence, we had decided to meditate individually, to see if we could reinitiate that feeling of tension and expectancy. As we did so, one of us had other ideas.

Producing a little unfolding table, a cereal bowl and a Tupperware box, one member decided it was time for breakfast. We meditated to the sound of crunching muesli.

This telling incident spelled the end of our vigil. Even Joeb seemed to have left Paul's psychic vicinity to avoid awkward questions. By 6.00am, we knew that our attempt to rendezvous with the circle-making forces had failed. Or, at least, almost failed. Three had been granted the sight of a ring of lights, as if something had thought about creating a formation and then decided not to. But this wasn't enough to compensate. We all felt we had been so close to witnessing a crop glyph appear in front of our eyes... Close, but not close enough.

Some were philosophical, others bitter and disappointed as we packed up our equipment in the gold of the early morning sunshine. Michael put a fatherly hand on our shoulders. He understood our frustration. Paul, understandably, took it the hardest. And *he* knew how the others felt from the rather bumpier ride he had back *down* the hill on the stretcher to the cars!

From there it was home to bed, to hide under the covers in depression and exhaustion.

The things some people do for metaphysics... Curious cows examine a group of very depressed adventurers descending from the hill, one in an old toddler buggy, stretcher now discarded. Photo: Barry Reynolds

The formation at Lancing which mutated on the night of our first rendezvous. The pattern of the original cross can be clearly seen through the overlaid circle. Photo: Michael Hubbard

Inside the Lancing cross very early in the morning after the rendezvous. The crop could only have gone down an hour or so before this picture was taken. The lay was unruly but intricate.

5: AFTERMATH AND REDEMPTION

A Cross Mutates

I didn't go straight home after the failed rendezvous. In an effort to cheer myself up, I decided to detour to Lancing where only the Friday before a crop formation had been discovered just below the A27 flyover across the River Adur. We were scheduled to do a full survey the following Monday but Barry had made a brief *recce* and had described it as a 'cross'; a small circle with four long arms emanating from the centre.

Under the grand gaze of Lancing College chapel, a local landmark which would play a role in our work the following year, I was puzzled when I reached the formation. What I was looking at was one large circle in very green wheat with four smaller ones bulging from it at each 'corner'. The lay wasn't neat but it seemed to be made up from many counter-rotating bands swirled in intricate layers. Could this be the cross-shaped pattern which Barry had been referring to? This wasn't my idea of a cross. Thinking little about it, I took some photographs and went home to much-needed sleep. I didn't know it then but I had just left the youngest formation I had ever been in.

The only known, sadly unspectacular, photograph of the Lancing cross before its mutation, showing a much smaller central circle. Taken from the nearby A27 flyover. Photo: Barry Reynolds

When I telephoned Barry later that day to mention my little venture, it was clear to him from my description that changes had taken place since he had photographed the shape from the flyover only the previous day. At the very time we were out freezing and meditating four miles or so north-east, this formation, the closest existing one to our rendezvous site, had mutated itself, the small central circle expanding outwards to cover the arms of the pattern, leaving just the end circles exposed. When I had entered it that morning, the new parts couldn't have been more than a few hours old.

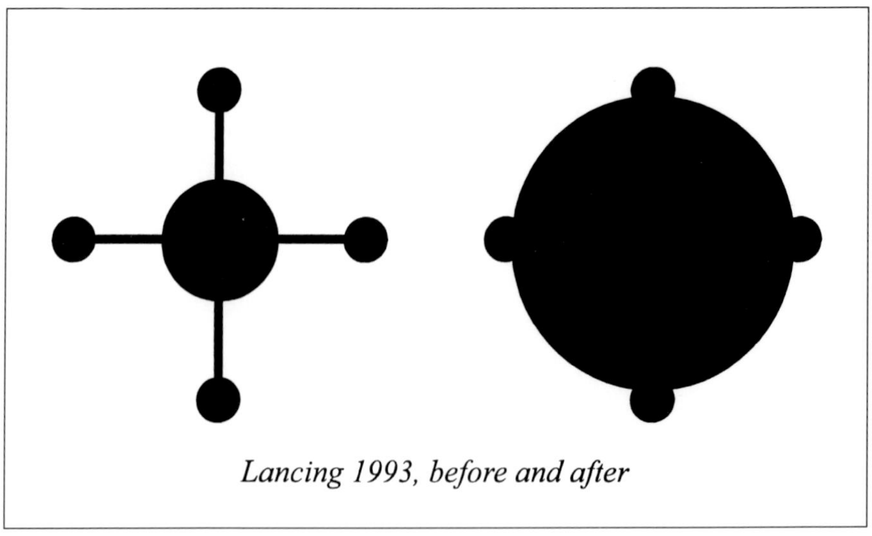

The 1993 crop formation at Lancing began life as the symbol on the left but only two days later became the shape on the right the night of the first rendezvous at Saddlescombe.

We immediately speculated the significance of this. Assuming this wasn't someone's idea of a joke - and if it was the timing was highly synchronistic - was this a sign from the circle-making forces that they were still around and active but that we were not yet deserving the experience of watching them work? Could it be they had popped down the road instead to give us just a little taster of what might have been, somewhere we would discover it, knowing it to have happened on 'our' night? Or were we simply being deluded by coincidence? There were more 'coincidences' to come which would suggest that our work on the 27th had more effect than we had at first suspected.

Psychic Dead-Ends

Of all the team, Paul's 'day after the night before' had been the most poignant and depressing. It was his psychic skills which had led to the concept of entering into this communication process in the first place and he felt as if he'd let the side down with the non-appearance of the crop formation the team had awaited for so long:

"To say I was depressed was a gross understatement. The sense of failure was so profound I wanted not just to disappear but emigrate to another planet. It was all my fault. I had been instrumental in bringing together all these people, all these excited, adventurous, intelligent people to a lone hillside in Sussex in the dead of night... and for what? A few glimpsed lights seen hovering over our field of barley. So what? Nothing meant anything to me anymore. Michael's friendly hand of consolation on my shoulder had done little to raise my spirits. I'd raised enough spirits that night and seen them plummet. Apart from anything else I was busting for a pee and the bumpy ride down the hill didn't help."

"Everything had come together like a well-rehearsed play. Every facet of information from the 'devil' vision to the energy line running though the pool and down into our field had been in place. Even the last small piece of information given by Carole, the vision of a fox, had been borne out. For me that signified that everything was right. We had been up and ready."

"This whole mess brought to mind another psychic dead-end that had occurred eighteen months before. I had been meditating on a regular basis with two friends, Greg and Kim. One evening, just as an experiment, I decided to see what psychic information we could pick up regarding the whereabouts of a sacred artefact in the area, one that had meaning and purpose to us. Closing my eyes I saw a small wood to my left by a river. In the wood was a large felled tree. The river curved 'round to the left and then to the right. Over it was a railway line. Greg got the name Epsom. I got out the Ordnance Survey map for Epsom in Surrey. Without any trouble I found the small wood. I also found a railway bridge running over the area, but no river!"

"Quenton and I decided to visit Epsom. The small wood dipped down into a valley, part of which was spanned by the railway bridge. A road meandered down toward the wood. I decided to make for the trees. But where was the river? This valley seemed to be built for a river! Then I saw it, the faint glimmer of running water. This was no river but a stream. "Oh well, I got it partly right," I mumbled to Quen. As we gazed at this small excuse for a river we spotted an old gentleman tending his lawn. "Excuse me," I said, "but is there a river around here?" "You're looking at it, mate," he replied. "That stream used to be a river before the Water Board got their hands on it. What you see is all that's left." Realising that we had found our river, every facet of the vision was in place, even the enormous felled tree. Yet even though guided by the Site Guardian of the place (we would learn more of Guardians later) we found nothing. At another date the Porthouse brothers helped in the search using shovels, dowsing rods and a metal detector. We dug and dug some more. (Well I didn't. I just shouted encouragement and provided hot soup.) Nothing! Why were we called there if there was nothing to be found!? I swore that one day I would return to try and find whatever it was that was buried there. This was an illustration of a seeming piece of psychic nonsense, a psychic dead-end!"

"But so many people were involved with the circle quest. I felt terrible. Quen and I drove back from Saddlescombe in silence. He didn't know what to say. Most of this stuff was new to Quenton even though we were very close. I felt I owed him an explanation. I didn't have one and remained mute. It wasn't even 7.00am yet, the sun was already high and we were hungry. We grabbed a fry-up at a transport cafe in Shoreham and then went off home to bed."

Paul's Redemption

Paul's attempts at rest weren't very successful. He had too much disappointment on his mind. But that Sunday night he was to receive a telephone call which was to brighten him considerably:

"I didn't sleep much. I got up around 2.00pm, came downstairs and read the papers. The gloom around me settled like a fog. I felt useless and extremely stupid, my mind only settling on the negative. Never mind that I had achieved some startling results in the past as a psychic. All that went out the window. I had failed miserably and I had nowhere to run to!"

"Then the phone rang. It was Tony Mezen, Jason and Mark's uncle and a fellow psychic friend of mine. "Paul," he said, "I thought you might be interested in what I saw last night." "What d'you mean?" I said, "What did you see?" Tony went on to tell me that at 2.15am (approximately the time we first gathered at the top of Saddlescombe) he had a terrible urge to go and sit in his garden. This he did. Between 2.15am and 4.30am Tony saw, flying over his house at Bexhill, East Sussex, no less than seventeen huge and glowing geometric shapes ranging from squares and oblongs to circles and triangles. This display of UFO phenomena was happening as we were all sitting looking at nothing! Tony had no idea of our project. We had kept the whole thing watertight. What he saw at exactly the time of our experiment blew away the fog that surrounded me. Light once more penetrated what was left of my shattered self-esteem. I knew with every atom of my being that what Tony saw was a message for us."

"The conditions on the hill were not right and therefore the circle-making forces could not comply. But they wanted us to know that it wasn't a waste of time, all was not lost. They smiled at us with the cosmic smile that only they could create... and I was going to live to fight another day."

Barry's Second Light

Barry took the failure of the previous night more calmly than some of the group and, after sleeping the morning off, spent the remainder of that Sunday much as any other weekend. At about 10.30pm, Barry and his wife Linda realised that their cat Edward had not yet come in for the night. Usually, he would reappear well before 10.00pm but tonight he had strayed further or for some reason hadn't felt the urge to return.

Standing in the garden from which Michael had seen his cluster of lights only twenty-four hours before, Barry called to Edward, with no response. As he did so, a feeling crept over him of some impending event about to occur. When nothing happened immediately he went inside and told Linda of his strange intuition. His instinct was that something significant might appear in the sky and he asked her to keep an eye out while he went for a shower. Linda, adrenaline now pumping, decided to wait in the garden for the cat and whatever else might happen...

Finishing his shower, clad only in a dressing gown, Barry suddenly felt the impulse to go straight downstairs and into the garden. Almost as soon as he got outside, Linda exclaimed "Look up there, what's that?". As they gazed, a bright white point came into view, like the brightest of stars, moving south-west to west. It was moving in a clearly defined arc across the sky. Barry and Linda watched the light for nearly three minutes as it executed a curving fly-past over their house. Then it was lost from view.

The pronounced arc of the light's movement ruled out its being a satellite and what with Burgess Hill being under several Gatwick airport flight paths Barry and Linda knew for a fact that this was no aeroplane or helicopter. The 'object' had been soundless. Given Barry and Michael's previous experiences and the lights seen at the rendezvous it seemed that again the involvement in psychic experiments had somehow coincided with, or generated, the appearance of light phenomena.

Andy Sees The Light

In the week following this anomalous sighting over Burgess Hill, I was to witness something similar myself.

As a musician, at this time I regularly recorded at my friend David Swingland's studio flat on the Wivelsfield side of Burgess Hill. One evening that week, at about 11.30pm, I was leaving for home, loading equipment into my car in a dark cul-de-sac. It was a gorgeous night, a full moon glowing across a pin-sharp clear sky. Closing the boot, I would normally step straight into the car and drive away. But this night I was struck by the need to wait and watch the sky for a while. Given recent events this wasn't such a strange thing to do but I didn't seriously expect to see anything.

Half a minute or so into my quiet vigil, coming from the north-west I suddenly saw a very intense light move steadily across the sky. On this moonlit night most of the stars were barely visible but this was burning bright. Astonishingly, following the first was another, smaller, point about three moon-widths behind (visually speaking). This seemed to be rapidly vibrating or wobbling, deviating slightly side to side from the dead-straight line of its brighter companion. At first I had taken the main light to be a satellite but the behaviour of its smaller pursuer ruled that out. No man-made object could oscillate that fast, however eccentric its path.

The satellite question was then thrown into relief by the arrival of what actually appeared to be one, heading south-west. Far dimmer than the very pronounced sparks passing overhead, its path actually crossed them and I was able to compare what I was seeing. From this, it was clear that the two strange lights were at a much lower altitude than the satellite but if they were in the Earth's atmosphere there was no sound.

After a few minutes the two fascinating glowing objects were lost from view behind the rooftops.

Confirmation And 'Coincidence'

I was not the only person to see these lights. In a curious 'coincidence', a word completely redundant by now, two people who would later play a part in our communication experiments also witnessed the same objects, completely independently and hundreds of miles from each other.

Down at Alton Barnes, Wiltshire, site of so many major crop formations over the years and Mecca to crop circle researchers, Steve Alexander, who would later become one of the most prominent photographers of the phenomenon, was part of a group camping in the field behind *The Barge* pub that night. One of the women present gazed up at the sky and muttered words to the effect of "I wish we could see a UFO". Almost immediately the same two lights that I was also witnessing flew across the sky to everyone's amazement. When Steve read my account of what I saw, in the crop circle journal *SC*, he telephoned me to confirm that his group had seen exactly the same things and observed identical effects. Steve was entirely open-minded to the idea of strange lights and UFOs; he himself had videoed a shining ball of luminescence hovering over fields and nearby crop formations at Milk Hill, Alton Barnes, in 1990, a piece of footage which had become very well known and much broadcast.

While this was going on, a young woman called Karen Douglas was part of an outside meditation held by the East Midlands branch of the Centre for Crop Circle Studies at Husbands Bosworth in Leicestershire. In their own efforts to communicate with the circle-making forces, they had only just sat down to concentrate when the two lights sailed overhead. In addition to confirming everything I and Steve's party had witnessed, Karen's group also reported that the smaller of the two objects attempted to overtake the brighter at one point before falling back into line.

That three separate parties saw the same phenomena at much the same time suggests that the lights were very high up and must have been seen by others. However, the uncanny aspect is that all three of us had a feeling beforehand that something was about to happen, as if we were being called specifically to witness them. Steve Alexander would later meet and fall in love with Karen Douglas and both would become part of the Sussex communication team...

Andy's Second Light

After the two lights had passed from my view I waited to see if anything else would transpire. All was quiet and after a while I set off home for Lewes, exhilarated and a little awed. As I drove, I began to feel uncomfortable and anxious, as if I was about to miss something. I watched the skies through the windscreen. On a whim I decided to cut across country through the village of East Chiltington. Almost without thinking, as I reached a gravel lay-by on a road which edged along a large wheat field, I found myself pulling in. Stepping out into the moonlit darkness I crossed the road and walked to an open entrance into the field.

My gaze alighted on a copse of trees on the opposite side of the field, silhouetted against the dark blue sky. Almost as soon as my eyes rested there, a very bright ball of light appeared out of nowhere directly above it. It hung in the air for several seconds, not moving. Suddenly, it dropped like a stone, vanishing behind the trees. I followed its descent through their trunks but it had gone, as if the Earth had quickly absorbed it.

I was shocked and amazed. For the second time in an hour I had been privileged to see for myself an anomalous light, the like of which I had often heard reported but never seen for myself. I had been clearly directed by some process to stand at this field and had been rewarded by something I didn't understand but somehow sensed I was meant to see. This seemed different to the first two lights though, as if they were definite 'objects' and this third one was more of an energy discharge. It must have been several feet across, judging from its apparent distance from the trees, and was certainly not a shooting star. It hung in the air for too long and had seemed to be only a hundred feet or so from the ground.

Though excited, I was by now feeling slightly unnerved, standing alone in the dark. I waited a little while longer, hoping, as always, that perhaps a huge crop formation might suddenly appear in front of me, but I was not to be treated tonight. Sensing that all was over, I returned to the car and drove home.

The Nature Of The Lights

What, if anything, was the meaning of the light phenomena experienced in the week before and after our first rendezvous? Could it be that through our interaction with psychic forces we had somehow become attuned to seeing other levels of reality which we normally wouldn't access on a visual level? There is evidence, from experiments carried out by researchers like Andrew Collins, that it is possible to generate light phenomena by the power of thought through the interaction of hitherto unknown energy sources. Carl Jung, in his 1959 book *Flying Saucers*, had

The field at East Chiltington where Andy witnessed the second of two anomalous light events on the same night. A white ball of luminescence appeared to hover over these trees before abruptly dropping out of sight.

previously put forward a similar idea but he believed many UFO sightings were products of the mind, visible only to the individuals perceiving them.

Yet if our lights were just projections of our own psychically-raised minds, how was it that the driver on the A23 had to stop to let Barry's object pass across the road? The first pair I saw were also seen by at least two other groups across the country that night, so there was little doubt that they were visibly present and not just to individuals - the strangeness here was that it seemed some of us were directed to witness them, in the same way that Barry and Linda were 'called' outside to wait for the sighting over their house. Michael had, of course, seen a cluster of lights from the same spot the night before. We didn't know if anyone besides Tony Mezen saw his seventeen geometric shapes going across the sky. Were they meant for him alone, the circle-making forces 'knowing' that he would transmit the knowledge of them back to us via Paul?

Perhaps, if they weren't random energy globules and there was any message at all behind these sightings, we were indeed being given tantalising glimpses of Devic beings or the raw energy that might be capable of creating our crop formation for us, as an incentive to continue the experiment. Or had we witnessed extra-terrestrial craft of some kind? Some of us suspected we had been close to gratification on the 27th June. Maybe we needed to fine-tune our methods and intent if our rendezvous attempts were to succeed, and the circle-making forces were just letting us know they were still around and aware of us. Whatever the real circumstances behind the lights, these and the mutation of the cross formation encouraged us to try the experiment again...

Wider shot of the field at East Chiltington, showing nearby farmhouses

A shot from Steve Alexander's famous video sequence of a ball of light at Alton Barnes, seen near the centre of the picture. This is very similar to what Barry and Andy witnessed on separate occasions.

The same sequence a few minutes later - here the light can be seen heading off at speed just above the centre of the picture, passing the tractor on the left. The driver saw and reported the light himself, without knowing it had been videoed by Steve. The event took place on 26th July 1990, around 4.30pm.

Another view of the pond at Saddlescombe to which we would return for a second rendezvous.

Barry tests one of the video cameras which were so important to our work in 1993.

6: TRY AND TRY AGAIN

Why The Failure?

Although the strange occurrences and visitations from balls of light were a contributing factor, even as some of us had struggled miserably down the hill from our first rendezvous attempt we suspected we might try a second. But before we could commit to such a venture we had to know exactly why the first had failed. Repeating the same mistakes wouldn't make much sense.

After the news of Tony's geometric shapes, the mutation of the cross, Barry's housecall from a UFO and my own encounters, a meeting with Joeb was hastily arranged with a view to setting up another rendezvous as soon as possible. The barley field at our chosen site wouldn't be there for much longer before the combine harvesters moved in.

As we suspected, Joeb confirmed there had been too much conflicting energy within the group. The Devic forces, we were told, didn't trust humankind at the best of times and could see the incohesion in the mix of our auric fields. If we weren't of the elusive 'one mind' at the most basic of levels, how could we be relied upon to present a video of such importance to the world with a united front?

A number of the participants had written down their feelings in the wake of the failed rendezvous and distributed them to the others. Carole informed us of a message she had received from her psychic communicator Shomas later on the 27th June:

"*There was so much energy there at one point, and yes, you did see misty entities floating before you, but the energy waxed and waned due to the negativity being produced. One held you all back and countermanded all the positive energy. We did advise it only needed one non-believer to spoil this thing. One weak link in the chain for it not to hold together. There will be another time, there will be further opportunities but choose your numbers more carefully. Screen the participants to ensure they won't fail.*"

Some of the group felt uncomfortable with the stance of singling out one person as being responsible for the failure of the whole project and disliked talk of "screening". In fairness, there had been a number of elements which were not quite right if we were entirely honest with ourselves. John Cole, in particular, believed this recriminatory approach wasn't fair. He wrote:

"*I felt strongly that this kind of direct contact approach was indeed the way forward and do so still. I do not accept, however... the proposed reason for the failure of the experiment. I find the idea that the doubt or scepticism of one or two members of the group was responsible pernicious, divisive and unlikely.*

It seems to me that beings more spiritually evolved than ourselves would understand the natural human tendency to doubt and question anything beyond our normal experience and would not punish us or refrain from communication with us just because we were unable to have complete faith in what they were channelling through to us. ...Anyone prepared to spend a cold night on a hillside without any sleep had as much faith in what we hoped would happen as can reasonably be expected. ...It is true that we all had our own approaches, hopes and motivations but to suggest that anyone had a primarily negative attitude is, to my mind, false.

It would also seem strange that, if our scepticism were the reason for failure, Joeb would not have mentioned it (at the time). *...I find the idea of purging the group of sceptics most distasteful and highly negative in itself.*

Without wishing to cast doubts on the genuineness of the channellers, I am afraid that my own feeling is that the channelling was unreliable. How do we know, after all, who or what we are communicating with when we listen to channelling? ...To believe that the information we receive through channelling is 100% reliable just because it is channelled is naive."

In truth, we had been aware all along that there was no way we could verify any of the channelling which came through. Part of the adventure was simply to take the information we received at face value to see whether any solid results would arise. We understood John's concerns but as scientific methods of trying to film the circle-making forces in action had not had any better success, most of us saw no reason not to continue using channelling as our guide for the time being, whatever it meant. Handy let out or not, Joeb himself had stated on several occasions that he could give no absolute guarantees of success. Understandably, Paul had a firmer acceptance of the validity of his contacts and the messages he was receiving.

Michael Green, who had been the key to sparking the idea for the communication project, felt a sense of responsibility toward the group and wrote a general letter to everyone, giving a deeper perspective into why the rendezvous might have failed but essentially agreeing that negativity on the part of some had been a problem:

"In this type of operation we are dealing effectively with spiritual realities, which have quite different ground rules. We are grappling with the problem of communication between two very different levels of reality, where intrusive negativity can be damaging to either party. An exceptionally high level of group bonding is required, with absolute dedication to a common ideal if successful results are to occur. Scepticism, a refusal to accept spiritual realities, self-interest and antagonism or resentment towards other group members all show up in the group aura. Negative auric signals are like red lights to the intelligences we are dealing with, who just shy away. It literally takes only one person, exhibiting negativity as an inward attitude in terms of anger or disbelief, to completely negate all the positive aspirations of the rest of the group.

The group must take a deep breath, gather its courage and learn from this experience. I suggest that you continue your group meditations and try and find out what people really believe and what their motivation is for belonging. Above all get to know and like each other better. Curiosity and companionship is not sufficient reason for belonging to such a group.

Paul, in particular, must not regard this setback in any way as a slight on his channelled material. Both it and he have been magnificent. I hope that later in the season you will try again with perhaps a smaller group. I think it is imperative that channelling occurs on site at the start of the operation and a check is made whether everybody has the right energies to be there. Group members who are out of harmony must have the grace to leave even at this late stage if this is necessary.

I am so sorry that the surveillance project on Saturday night was such a cruel disappointment after all the work and hopes that the group had put into it. However, we must not let one unfortunate operation become a serious setback. Above all it should not become the occasion for recriminations and ill feeling. Everyone who participated did their very best by their lights."

Despite, or perhaps because of, these serious thoughts in our minds, there seemed no reason not to make another attempt. With this understanding of why we might have failed, we decided to go for second time lucky.

Another Try

With all the requisite channelling and guidance from Joeb, who assured us, with caution, that it was worth pursuing, we agreed to set up another rendezvous. This time though, we couldn't wait for any psychic visions of dates and times - the fields would be coming down before too long and many of the group had upcoming summer holidays booked! The circle-making forces would have to agree to our schedule. *Where* to hold the event was never in doubt - we would return to the same site as before, which had been visualised so firmly by the three clairvoyants. The early hours of Sunday 3rd July was the only date which could be agreed between the team and Joeb confirmed that this would be acceptable.

Quietly, we decided to pare the group down a little. It seemed clear from reactions on the night of the first experiment and from correspondence afterwards, who would be willing to give the enterprise another try. Ted had always seemed uncomfortable with his involvement and John, friend and colleague though he was, had made clear his reservations about the set-up. As a result, they weren't asked to take part in the second rendezvous, cruel as it seemed. More difficult was the issue of whether or not to invite Michael to participate again. Although he had been one of the main initiators of the project and was always welcomed, we all felt a responsibility towards him to come up with a tangible result, creating a pressure that wasn't entirely conducive to total positivity. We needed to see if we could succeed on our own, without one of our chief mentors present. Reluctantly, we decided not to ask Michael although he would return for future projects. We did, however, decide to include Barry's wife Linda as a way of making up a better balance of male and female energies.

The arrangements for 3rd July were virtually the same as before - and with them came the same obstacles. Once again we had to stretcher Paul up the hill, together with mounds of equipment, in the darkness of the pre-dawn hours. With three less men to help, even more journeys were necessary to shuttle everything up to the top. As if this were not draining enough, another problem raised its head.

A few days before, Diana called to say she was undergoing a minor operation that week. She would not be badly incapacitated - but would be unable to climb the hill to the site on the 3rd. Desperate not to be left out of the proceedings, she wanted to know if there was a solution. There was only one thing for it - in addition to Paul, we would have to stretcher Diana up to the top too...

If this sounds ludicrous now (and it does), it at least shows how dedicated we were to achieving our goal. Despite our first disappointment, there was still a real feeling that with the lessons learned we could be successful this time.

The down side of all this stretchering and lumping of equipment was that by the time we finally settled, we were in a completely debilitated heap. Nevertheless, in a change from our first attempt, we opened proceedings with a short ritual. Each member had been asked by Joeb to bring a small offering of flowers from their garden or a favourite place as a small dedication to the 'Spirit Guardian' of the site. Guardians, we were told, were entities which looked after the energies of certain areas of land. We would learn much more about them in 1994.

Unfortunately, there was one more journey down the hill to be made. An hour or so after our vigil began, what we had feared on the 27th June came to be realised - our procession of cars parked in the farmer's track at the bottom attracted attention. At about 3.30am we observed a car draw up on the main road. Figures with torches got out and began to examine our vehicles. Fearing that we were about to become the victims of thieves, a number of us leapt to our feet and hared down the hill again, in the hope of reaching the cars before all was too late... When we got about two-thirds of the way down, we realised that the intruder vehicle was a patrol car. The police had become interested in our stationary convoy. Relieved that at least our cars weren't about to be broken into, we observed what happened. As luck would have it, they decided not to pursue their discovery and, after sniffing around, drove off again. But this left us with another journey back up the hill...

On top of our physical depletion, the weather was not so kind to us this night. Low cloud began to roll in and soon the faint lights of distant Brighton became lost to us as a heavy blackness descended, bringing with it a light drizzle. Cold and damp, we waited, but our spirits weren't high. The legacy of Diana's operation was causing her discomfort and she was concerned that the bat which had been flitting around us earlier might be a symbol of negativity. There was even a tangible buzz of bad feeling between two of our members; they had argued earlier in the evening and the dust clearly hadn't settled yet. Some of us grew very cold and extremely tired. Any Devic forces observing our auras would not have been impressed if they were searching for signs of total positivity. Diana had a vision which illustrated this:

"I saw misty shrouds in the field - then I saw quite clearly a group of spiritual beings watching us - one seemed to be surrounded by others each side of him. Towards the end he gestured towards us with his hand as if to say 'Sorry! But it is up to you to get it right!'"

As the night wore slowly on, no unusual lights were seen and no surges of energy made us rush to the cameras, although we did activate them from time to time just in case. It became harder to keep all the videos operating after a while because their automatic dew protection facilities were coming on in response to the fine rain. Perhaps it's just as well that by the time the grey and unwelcoming dawn finally came up, nothing had happened. The ultimate irony would have been for our formation to have suddenly appeared in a dizzying flurry of moving lights and for none of the cameras to have worked.

With heavy hearts, we realised that once again we had failed.

The Canvas Lost

The week or so after this monumentally disappointing event was a predictable round of depression, further channelling and soul-searching. We didn't need any psychic information to tell us why the second attempt had failed. We all knew that the feeling on the night hadn't been up to scratch. We had physically exhausted ourselves to get everyone and everything up onto the hill and hadn't recovered in time to be of any use in projecting positive energy. The weather had been disheartening and some of the strained relations between certain group members were far from ideal. In a letter from Diana to the group, she wrote:

"The bat was a symbol of negativity around us. Also, I was not happy at one person smoking - after all, what does smoke do but pollute the atmosphere?"

Clearly, we had not been in any fit state to convince the circle-making forces that we were ready for the experience of watching them work. In the aftermath of the second attempt, this time there were no hopeful signs or strange lights to encourage us to continue. Perhaps we had been given up on. Keeping so many people all of one mind was proving to be an impossible task. If we were to try the experiment again we would have to decrease the numbers further and re-think our strategy.

In the week after this second disappointment, the news came through - our field of barley had been harvested. After all the work in finding the exact spot for the rendezvous, our ideal site was now useless to us. If we were going to try one more time we would have to move fast and find a new canvas for the circle-making forces to work in.

The weird 'kebab' formation at Sompting, complete with arrowhead pointing towards Paul's house. This was the site for our third and final rendezvous attempt.

A Night In A Kebab

Despite our frustration at not succeeding with the experiment, we could hardly accuse the circle-making forces of having deserted us. 1993 had seen a massive burst of crop formation activity in the Sompting-Lancing area (detailed in *Fields of Mystery*), started with the triangular triplet which had inspired us a just a few weeks earlier but which now seemed so long ago. We had spent so much time surveying these formations yet it seemed to escape us that while we were trying to make crop circles appear at circleless Devil's Dyke, Sompting was having a bonanza. Were our contacts on the other side of this dimension trying to tell us something?

With our chosen field now useless stubble, it made sense to move operations to where everything was happening. Once again there was no time to wait for psychic visions; we would have to dictate the time and the place.

On 23rd June, the same night that a huge 'celtic cross' design appeared in an adjacent field, a small circle in wheat with two short emanating pathways was discovered. David Russell, an experienced dowser and a friend of the group, instinctively felt, from the energy patterns he could detect, that this small design would grow. He was right. On the nights of the 29th and 30th June, the circle suddenly developed into a long line of

The view from the kebab; from here we would have clear sight of a crop formation appearing if our experiment was successful.

strange shapes in a chain. Its final bizarre look earned it the nickname 'the kebab'. Though some suspected that parts of the last additions may have been man-made, one aspect of the design seemed to be a good omen. An arrowhead triangle at the south of the pattern seemed to point directly to Paul's house just half a mile or so away.

With this area of Sompting so active and the kebab so lively with growth spurts, it was decided, without much debate, to hold the third rendezvous actually within this formation which seemed to suggest a link with Paul's home. The view from the kebab was promising - the same field dipped sharply and then back up again, following the direction of the arrowhead looking south, giving an elevated position on which to look down on the crop. Our cameras would be able to detect a pattern appearing with no trouble. The kebab almost signposted "Try here!". This seemed to be another ideal spot; even the farmer was friendly and had given his permission for us to carry out any experiments we wanted that year. Conversation with Joeb confirmed the circle-making forces' assent. A date was set for the early hours of 25th July.

Paul saved us a hard decision. Although the kebab was a more accessible place in which to congregate, heaving him into the field was not going to be easy. But Paul himself decided that this time he would sit the night out, bodily at least. Recognising that our physical depletion wasn't helpful to positive thought energy, he would spend the hours tuning in from his house nearby. The channellings which had actually been carried out on site at the previous two occasions had generally been ones of gentle guidance rather than hard information. We would be able to manage without our 'hotline' and in any case would have Diana and Carole with us as our psychic guides. Linda, Adam and Quenton also decided to drop out of the experiment for reasons of their own.

The five of us remaining, Barry, Martin, Diana, Carole and myself, despite all the adversity, still believed passionately that we could be successful, and there was no question that - this time! - we really were all of one mind. The group had whittled itself down naturally to a core of people who shared the same general thoughts and were open to receiving such an experience as that we desired. We gathered at Diana's house in Dorking, Surrey, a week before the experiment as a way of preparing ourselves properly with meditation and frank exchanges to avoid falling into the pitfalls of the second attempt.

On the 24th July we received a call from Carole. She had gone down with flu and wouldn't be fit to join the team. We would have to go ahead with just four of us. The male/female balance would be rather uneven, but we would have to cope.

Of all the three rendezvous attempts, this was the most harmonious. It was a glorious, still night, a canopy of stars shining brightly above us. A heavy dew came down later, but we were prepared and unbothered by the damp. Sitting in the original circle of the kebab formation, we each held a crystal which we had chosen at Diana's house. She had laid out a number of different shape and size and asked us to take the one which felt right. With these crystals in our palms, led by Diana, we meditated at intervals in a more structured way than before. With just four people it was easier and more appropriate to focus our thoughts in this way, in a ring, hands linked together. Everyone was relaxed and in good spirits. Paul, sitting alone upstairs in the house of the saucers, sent out his thoughts to us - in-between fighting off sleep!

The night had been so pleasant, it seemed almost churlish to complain that no formation had appeared by the time the golden morning light was shining. We felt a little disillusioned but not the bitter depression of the last two occasions. This time there could be no accusations that any negativity had passed between us or that we had been putting out anything other than the right 'vibes' to any Devic forces which may have gathered around us. We felt we had done our best. If the experiment had not worked this time, then it was never going to - at least not with the methods we were using.

"Don't take issue with the circle-makers...". Our view of the Mill Hill pictogram as we contemplated the reasons for the third rendezvous failure.

Taking Issue

As we drove back from the kebab in Barry's car, we decided to detour to take a passing look at an insect-like pictogram which had appeared at Mill Hill near Shoreham a couple of weeks before. Sitting in the car, Diana received a clear psychic impression of what had gone wrong that night - she was told that the experiment should not have taken place *inside an existing crop formation*. Had a new shape appeared in the same field, any glyphs in the immediate vicinity, linked by energy lines, would have been activated instantaneously by the same power used to lay the crops down. Diana was told that this force, whilst not generally harmful, should not be felt at close quarters in its most active state. Given the experience of Vivien and Gary Tomlinson, the couple in Surrey who had circles appear around them, we could believe that, but I was angry.

Why had Joeb or any of our other-worldly communicants not warned us of this effect *before* the event? They had been fully aware of our intentions yet didn't seem to have been told by the circle-making forces, who they claimed to have contacts with through their various levels, that to sit inside the kebab would be prohibitive to the experiment working.

"I have to take issue with that," I said, when I heard Diana's psychic disclaimer. No-one could explain why this information hadn't been imparted before and to me it just felt like an excuse. Martin sidled up to me as we gazed down upon the Mill Hill pictogram and said, in a humorously sinister voice, "*Don't* take issue with the circle-makers..." At this, some of my anger dissolved and I had to laugh. Martin was right. There we were getting annoyed at forces utterly beyond our comprehension, unknowable minds capable of creating huge and fantastic patterns in our fields by methods no-one could explain. How could we possibly know what conditions or specifications were necessary for them to perform? Despite Joeb's description of the processes involved in the creation of crop formations there was no way of verifying the truth. We had made a stab at interacting with these elusive forces, with some intriguing results, but if they remained distant and unreachable, who was I to get irritated with them?

Nevertheless, this third failure raised some serious questions about the level of communication we were attaining. I didn't doubt Paul, Diana or Carole's psychic abilities but it was clear that the use of channelling to set up arrangements with circle creators was never going to be entirely reliable. Because humans *were* fallible, as the mouthpieces for the channelled messages, it could never be one hundred percent certain. With this in mind, our sources needed to be as pure and powerful as possible. If we were going to continue with this kind of work we would have to find a being with a higher level of knowledge than Joeb, wise and noble though he appeared to be.

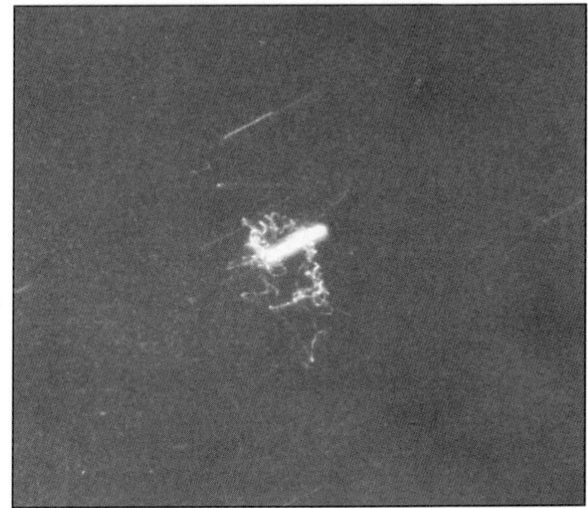

The only anomalous light which appeared in connection with our work to be captured on camera. The best of eight different photographs, this extraordinary image was taken by a friend of Barry's (who wishes to remain anonymous) at Burgess Hill while we were meditating in the kebab formation. The frame was taken on a time exposure of about five minutes, hence the long 'streaking' of the light (other faint streaks are stars). The long exposure has caught one of the abrupt movements of the object, which shows up as the squiggly lines visible here. The picture was taken on a Canon AE1 Program camera, mounted on a tripod, with a 200mm lens, using 400ASA film, probably at F8 or F11.

More Signs In The Sky

There was one glint of encouragement from the kebab meditation. In a similar situation to Tony Mezen experiencing UFO activity on the night of our first rendezvous, at the exact time we were opening our vigil in the formation a friend of Barry's was photographing a bright object in the sky over Burgess Hill, very like that which Barry and Linda had seen a few weeks before. A local businessman, he suddenly felt compelled to look out of his back window just as he was preparing for bed. He spotted the light about 1.00am and watched it for at least an hour. Though predominantly white, its colour seemed to fluctuate to pale green and red occasionally. The glowing object sat motionless in the sky for several minutes at a time before abruptly conducting sharp looping acrobatics and returning to its original point again. A keen photographer, the duration of the sighting enabled Barry's friend to set up his camera. Using very long exposures he managed to capture the light trails of this movement on eight frames (see photograph). Only a week before, on hearing of Barry's own previous experiences with anomalous lights, this friend had exclaimed "Well, what you need is photographic evidence". A week later, he had it himself.

Was this sighting, again, a little message to us via secondary sources that success was still possible and that we shouldn't give up the quest?

In the immediate days after, on a visit to Alton Barnes in Wiltshire, site of so many major crop glyphs in the past, Martin, his friend 'Griller' Gilgannon and I witnessed an eerie sight the memory of which will probably stay with us for the rest of our lives. In the very early hours of 27th July - exactly a month since the first rendezvous - we were 'crop watching' from our car at the foot of East Field (home to most of Alton Barnes' major formations) at about 4.15am on a very gloomy morning. I had fallen asleep in the back and Griller was dozing in the front when we were woken by Martin's anxious voice calling us to consciousness. As my eyes snapped open I could see through the windscreen, directly in front of us, what he was seeing. With just a hint of dawn light silhouetting Golden Ball Hill ahead, ominously and bizarrely, huge flickering 'blocks of darkness' were passing swiftly in front of the downland ridge from left to right at an incredible speed which seemed to give a strobe effect. These moving shadows appeared to cover the entire expanse of the hill as they flew but were certainly not clouds. Martin got out of the car for a clearer look but I was gripped by a strange fear which held me inside. After a minute or so, the dark objects faded from view. It was as if the blocks - which was the only description we could put on what we saw - were something not quite in this dimension. They were very definitely *there* yet seemed to lack physical substance in a way which suggested we had been granted a very brief window into something outside our normal existence and utterly beyond our comprehension. What these were was impossible to say. The following night, up on the ridge of downs itself, we observed pale green orbs of light floating high above the Vale of Pewsey...

The Heeding Of The Widows

As for continuing the communication project in 1993, three disappointments in one summer were enough for all of us. The combine harvesters were hard at work in the fields of Sussex and very soon no crops would be left standing. There was neither the time nor the inclination left to pursue another rendezvous. Any further work would need serious reconsideration of how to go about it and family members of those in the group were beginning to feel left out and neglected. Circle season was always hectic at the best of times for those out actively seeking and surveying formations and the wives and girlfriends of some of the male members of the team had christened themselves the 'Crop Circle Widows'... Yet more days and nights out would hardly have been tactful.

The Widows' concerns about the sanity and commitment of their male partners had been amusingly illustrated the year before, when some of them were dragged to an all-night wait at the foot of the prehistoric mound Silbury Hill in Wiltshire on a dodgy tip-off that something amazing was going to happen (it didn't). Cold and miserable by three o'clock, the voice of Martin's fiancee Sloane rose dryly through the darkness: "Martin. I'm leaving you". It was meant as a joke, but we all took the point.

Spire of St Mary's at Sompting, central focus for the jurisdiction of a discarnate being we came to know as 'Cened'.

7: SEEKING THE GUARDIANS

A New Approach

As the autumn of 1993 took the leaves off the trees and the implications of the work we had carried out over the summer sank in, our thoughts began to turn to the forthcoming circle season. Should we attempt once again to set up a date to video a crop pattern appearing? If so, after recent failures, we would have to re-evaluate how to go about it.

We could continue to use Joeb as our main go-between and might eventually get a result, but there was a feeling, even intimated by Joeb himself, that we needed to get in touch with a psychic entity on much closer terms with the circle-making forces. Maybe we had pushed Joeb to the limits of his abilities. He stressed on many occasions that just because he existed on a higher dimensional plain than us, this did not give him unlimited knowledge. There were many other levels above him. Clearly we were not receiving all the information we needed for success; we had to reach out to those more advanced levels.

Guardian Insurance

At the second rendezvous, Michael and Joeb had suggested we make an offering to the 'Site Guardian' of the area as a mark of respect and we had taken flowers. A belief in the concept of 'Guardians' permeates many cultures and religions. To increase the chances of achieving our goal in 1994, Michael advised us that perhaps we needed to integrate them more closely into our work. He wrote:

"I hold myself responsible for not stressing this point earlier before the group carried out the surveillance programme last summer - indeed, this omission may have been a major factor in the failure of the operation."

Maybe we were trying to monopolise the energies and Devic forces of an area without asking the permission of the Guardian whose job it was to co-ordinate these aspects within a designated area. Paul describes the role of the Guardians as he sees it:

"Part of a Guardian's work is indeed to guard. That is, they are caretakers of a certain area of land, they help co-ordinate the various forces of nature used in the growing of crops and the maintenance of rocks and minerals. Not in the physical sense but in a very subtle etheric sense. If you accept that everything is part of everything else and therefore if you upset a part of that system you upset the *whole* system, no matter how slight that may be, then you begin to understand the work of a Guardian. He or she maintains the Earth's subtle energy lines. These lines need to be kept clear so that vital power can get through to all areas of the planet, nourishing and sustaining it in much the same way as meridian lines in the human body. In fact the human body and the Earth are very similar. The Earth has 'chakric' energy points just like a human being. It also has chakric systems *within* chakric systems *un*like human beings. And just as we can get sick when one or more of our meridian lines gets blocked, so then does the Earth and it is part of the Guardians' work to keep them clear - but with human beings about, especially at this particular time in history, this gets harder and harder and their work-load is enormous."

"The negativity that modern humans create is awesome, mainly because they no longer believe that the Earth is a living, thinking, feeling entity. That being so, they now kick seven bells out of it with poison, rape and theft. Look what happens to a human when it gets poisoned, raped or is stolen from: the body gets sick, the mind gets sick, emotions get sick. So it is with the Earth. She DOES feel sick, she DOES feel trauma and pain and, like humans, she cries for help, sometimes in the form of the signals she creates on the surface of her body, usually in cereal crops. Where food is, people are, and they can see."

"Guardians work closely with the Devic forces but in no way 'control' them. The Devas work *with* them, not *for* them and these little ones, who have come to so mistrust and dislike human beings, work with the Guardians because they choose to do so, knowing that in them they have an ally."

"Not all Guardian work is to do with Earth maintenance. As I understand it, some look after holy sites that need protecting from violation by human beings. Although they can sometimes show themselves, or at the very least make themselves 'felt', there is little they can do to prevent desecration, but they sometimes manage to scare the hell out of people."

"There are other types of Guardians but that which is more prevalent than any other is our OWN personal one. We all have them whether we like it or not. Every human on this planet has a 'spirit guide'. Usually they have known us for many, many life-times, often having been a blood relative during our many lives. They guide our spiritual welfare, or try to. We don't always listen or sense that they are there and most people are not taught that they exist, but a subtle prompting on an inner level seems to be the norm and many people have experienced their 'Guardians' in some way, shape or form. Joeb is mine!"

We would learn later that the areas of Guardian jurisdiction were often triangular in shape. However, some regions had no spiritual presence at all, particularly where too much negativity had been created by humans, either environmentally or spiritually at scenes of extreme disasters and atrocities; some things, it seemed, were too much for them to cope with. The being called Cened, who we would speak with later, told us that Guardians were not always present at their post and spent time on other activities elsewhere. He would come when called to duty by a mysterious 'Council' or when humans requested his presence: *"One voice calls me and I am here"*.

The vast Iron Age hill-fort of Cissbury Ring, a massive source of earth energy and home to the three Guardians 'Emun', 'Rachael' and 'Tryst'. Photo: John Holloway

We clearly needed to contact the Guardians in charge of the areas we intended to carry out any further experiments in. But as there were no firm plans about where and when to plan the next rendezvous we really had to talk to one *before* deciding what to do. Where to start?

Cissbury Ring

From the explosion of crop circle activity in the Sompting region which began seriously in 1992 (a lone pictogram was found there in 1990), several of the dowsers we were in contact with had asserted that the central power point of the earth energy utilised to create them seemed to be Cissbury Ring, a mile or so north west.

An ancient Iron Age hill-fort, one of the largest in Britain, crafted from an outcrop of the South Downs, Cissbury was held as a very sacred place in local folklore and had been the site of settlements and flint mines from as early as c.3,500 BC before its distinctive ramparts were shaped around 250 BC. Curiously, legend holds that Cissbury was created at the same time as Devil's Dyke when the Devil himself fought with St Dunstan...

A major energy line, the dowsers told us, came down from Cissbury and flowed directly into St Mary's, the old Knights Templar Church at Sompting. From here, the energy appeared to splay outwards like rays to create the crop formations which surrounded it. There seemed no better starting point in our Guardian hunt than Cissbury Ring.

A Demon-Haunted World

Even so, we felt we had better beware. A number of spooky stories surrounded this mysterious place, which suggested that beings might be present which were not all benevolent, as Paul explains:

"A good dowser friend of mine, Hilda Bell, told me a story that occurred about twelve years before when a group from the Lancing area decided to have a day out dowsing Cissbury Ring. There are old flint mines up there and the place is a positive power-house of energy lines, feeding into tumuli, sacred mounds and pre-reformation churches. Whilst practising their craft with pendulums and rods, one of the group plunged a stick into the ground. From it rose a huge demonic-looking beast complete with horns. With a shriek the bold little band of dowsers were sent running down the hill for all they were worth as if the hounds of hell were in pursuit, which, as far as they were concerned, was not far off the truth. It appeared to chase them for a little while then disappeared. As far as I know it was never seen again."

"This type of Guardian, Joeb told us, was no more than a gigantic thought-form, a holographic image, created by adepts of old religions. These metaphysical masters were expert at creating 'programmed' thought-forms by a process of the mind. When triggered, these monsters appear as real as their creators intended, often complete with sound, wailing and roaring. The more intelligent ones are capable of actual speech. This same type was used by the Egyptians to guard their tombs. A truly terrible thought-form can so terrify a person as to cause them harm. But usually the energy used to create these images of terror is soon dissipated when sparked more than once, though to the recipient once is one too many!"

The Cissbury Guardians

We decided to make our way to Cissbury one morning, to see if it would be possible for Paul to channel any entities present there. But before setting out, we needed to do some homework. By psychically tuning in, using dowsing if necessary, Paul felt it should be feasible to determine the number, nature and even name of the Cissbury Guardians from his house. We would then be better prepared for an actual meeting with whatever and whoever we would find. He discovered that there were three; 'Emun', 'Rachael' and 'Tryst':

"After my initial tune-in to Emun (pronounced *Ee-moon*), a male entity, he started feeding me information regarding his fellow Guardians. Surprisingly, they were both female. Surprise because, in my experience, female Guardians are rare, though they are very often found where a holy well is sited, or a healing spring. But here was not one female but two! Tryst represented the Earth Mother and Rachael (pronounced *Rack-ale* - this name was as near a pronunciation as I could get) represented the sun. Emun represented the moon. Rachael had an 'Egyptian' feel about her yet she was not obviously Egyptian. She carried an image of the sun around her neck. She was very beautiful and, like Tryst, very feminine. Tryst looked like someone out of biblical times, a haunting Jewishness about her; she was dark and quite delightful to look at. Emun wore some sort of robe and carried a staff with a crescent moon mounted on its tip. He was full-bearded. It became clear that they served a deity of some kind and that they all functioned together."

On 12th December 1993 five of us, Paul, Barry, Linda, Martin and myself, set out for Cissbury Ring. The plan had been to make our way to the top on one of the footpaths which wound up to it, Paul in his trusty wheelchair, but one look at the weather was enough to scupper this plan. Heavy clouds and sheets of rain hid the Ring from view. Paul reckoned that we shouldn't give up; close proximity to the site might be enough to enable him to make contact with the Guardians.

Driving to the lower of two car parks which edged up to Cissbury Ring, a popular beauty spot, we halted in the middle of what would normally be busy with cars, people and dogs on a Sunday morning. Perhaps luckily, in terms of avoiding drawing attention to ourselves, the heavy rain deterred even the hardiest adventurers and we were the only ones present. Crammed into Paul's not-very-large vehicle, we held our first ever car park meditation. We didn't know for sure whether anyone would speak through Paul or if it was it even possible to channel a Guardian. We soon had our answer. In the hope that we would be successful it had only dawned just before setting out that we should bring a tape recorder with us to capture the moment. The only device to hand was Barry's son's colourful and clumpy 'Toys-R-Us' kiddie cassette machine. With this honourable offering held up to Paul's mouth as he tuned in, we awaited our first contact with a Guardian.

The first words weren't promising. An almost imperceptibly quiet, dry, ancient voice which sounded as if it hadn't spoken the English language for aeons grated "*What do you want?*". The tone was almost gruff, resentful. Of the three Guardians Paul had discerned, we had picked up Emun (or 'Ahmon' - an Egyptian name - as Michael spells it). As we learned later, Guardians have little reason to trust or converse with humans any more than Devas do. It was an honour that he had deigned to speak at all.

We explained the nature of our work to this remarkable being, whose presence gradually grew stronger and warmer. More used to speaking with disembodied entities than the others, I generally acted as spokesperson in these sometimes difficult conversations. But, once aware of what we were after - help with our project to video a crop formation appearing - Emun surprised us by disowning any knowledge of the circle-making process. They were aware, he said, of the patterns appearing on their land and of the Devas' role in their creation but they played no part themselves. Emun would later tell us that the Devas were mischievous and elusive even to him. Devas were so different from ourselves - and indeed the Guardians, generally discarnate humans who once lived in our physical dimension - that they were difficult to converse and interact with even at Emun's level of existence. Guardian's main functions seemed to be ensuring the smooth flow of life energy through the Earth and governing the welfare of plants and animals within their areas. Emun explained his position:

"If you are asking whether I can give you a blessing for the crop circles, I cannot give you that. This is out of our jurisdiction. But what we can do is, when you set up your time, we will make sure that the energy lines are set up correctly. ...We know that you come in search of knowledge, to be able to interpret what these circles are to many, many people. We have had circles before, this is not new. They come at odd times; they would come occasionally for various sections of people in this country, in this England. For special times they would be created. These were moments of great joy for the peoples they would come to instruct. Now they come to instruct the world... but we are not involved with this. But we will help you as best we can. When you have established through other communications where the circle will be, or could be, we will do our best to ensure that the energy is pure and free."

As Emun spoke, he seemed to be tapping energy from all of us in the car, as if drawing strength from our life force to enable him to communicate, an effect noted before with psychic phenomena. We were all struck with a sudden weariness - that was not boredom! - as he spoke. Barry, sitting directly behind Paul, felt particularly drained.

Emun went on to express his concern that Cissbury Ring itself was being threatened with destruction. A proposed by-pass extension of the A27 threatens to carve directly through it, as other sacred sites of England have been wilfully demolished to make way for wastelands of consumerism and our new god - the motor car. Only government cutbacks currently hold this scheme at bay. After his initial reluctance, Emun seemed pleased that someone was aware of the Guardians of Cissbury at last because it might draw attention to the plight of the Ring itself:

"We are here to help with the various forces of nature here, including humankind. We are here to create harmony. ...But we have no power against the humans. We have no power in preventing what they do. We can only send down thought-energy that they might change their mind over what they are doing. But the more people who are interested in Cissbury and know that this small section of land is a living entity, the better it is."

Despite the potential usefulness of having made contact with one of the Cissbury Guardians, as far as getting closer to the circle-making forces went we were no better off. From what Emun had told us, it didn't seem as if he was particularly upset that we had carried out experiments without consulting them. It would be worth our while tracking down others of his kin but it clearly wasn't going to give us the answers we needed. Nevertheless, Emun indicated his willingness to speak with us again and suggested that now Paul had made initial contact, he might be able to channel him from home.

At Home With Emun

Paul found that indeed, albeit with difficulty, now he had tuned in to Emun's 'frequency' it was possible to channel him without physically being at Cissbury. The Guardian was often weak though and would sometimes fade from Paul's consciousness in the middle of speaking - a stark contrast to Joeb who boomed loud and clear.

As the weeks passed and 1994 arrived, Paul slowly filtered information from Emun, who began to understand more clearly our need for a higher source of psychic

It wasn't that unusual for Paul's customers to find him dowsing for ancient temples and women's naked bellies… (Video image)

information and apparently realised how he could perhaps be of help to us with this. At the same time, Paul began to have strange visions...

"I was receiving information regarding Cissbury Ring that made no sense. I was being shown the belly of a naked woman. No sexual fantasy here. I knew the difference and rose above the chortles of my trusty fellows. I felt strongly that the hill-fort and this female form were linked. I got out the Ordnance Survey map for some name that might give me a clue like 'Belly Ridge' or 'Navel Way'. But nothing! Nothing came remotely near. The next image was of a temple I was told once stood on top of Cissbury Ring. I managed to get an aerial-view map of the Ring: it had the shape of a large footprint or... the shape of a woman's naked torso! And, sure enough, the dowsing pendulum indicated very strongly that a temple had indeed once stood on exactly the navel region of my naked lady. The female influence was strong indeed."

"I asked my good friend and excellent dowser David Russell to check my findings. Not only did he confirm them but he found that the temple (to the goddess Diana) was built on top of a far more ancient site where once stood a twelve foot high sarsen stone. We dowsed that this was at least 8000 years ago! Although this was questionable in terms of Neolithic history this information came through very strongly and when David got information that flowed quickly and unasked for (he was only dowsing for the site of a temple) he was usually right, as he was in predicting the mutation of the kebab formation at Sompting the year before. It would appear that the old stone, which I 'christened' the 'Navel Stone', was broken up by the Romans and used as a foundation for the temple to Diana."

"Later, Emun told us that he and the other Guardians used to serve the old chieftains and shamens of long ago when they would sit in silent communion around the Navel Stone. Part of their work as Guardians, he told us, was local weather control and care of crops. But they also helped set up communication with "*the Gods*", an input of wisdom for that ancient community of people. He went on to tell us that we could make contact with a higher intelligence that would be able to help us via the fifth energy band of the etheric remnants of the standing stone, that is the 'memory image' of the stone that was still dowsable. The fifth band is one of seven layers of energy found curled around some ancient standing stones. The fifth band is that of 'communication' corresponding with the throat chakra of human beings; indeed ALL the bands correspond with the human chakric system, the auric energy opening points on our bodies. I understood that this higher contact must take place on the 28th June 1994 between 2.00pm and 4.00pm. Emun was very specific but he had no idea whatever as to who or what we would communicate with. When that communication eventually took place its power and sense of intelligence would nearly take my head off!"

None of us really knew what we were expecting to happen on this newly divined date - a year and a day from our first rendezvous - but it looked like we were about to get our closer contact to the circle-making forces after all. What would happen? Would we be surrounded by glowing Devic beings or a have a close shave with an extra-terrestrial craft? Or would this, as was more likely, be a channelling with a far higher being than that we were used to, giving us the secret knowledge we needed to make our experiments work? Emun wouldn't - or couldn't - say. All he would stress was that we had to be at the top of Cissbury Ring on the site of the Navel Stone at the date and time specified:

"*28th June is a date when the stars and the moon and the Earth are in a certain movement and you will be able to communicate with the Higher Spheres at this particular time. It can be done in the afternoon between two and four o'clock. If you will co-operate, we will be there. First you must find where the stone stood, then you must sit around it… in a circle. There you will find the fifth band. This man* (Paul) *will then tune into the fifth band and with your help and meditation we shall see what happens, I can do no more. Then it is out of my hands.*"

At least this time we wouldn't have to struggle up hills in the middle of the night and Cissbury Ring had clearly defined footpaths up which we could wheel Paul. Still, we needed to do a recce of the vicinity first to work out our best strategy and to find the exact location of the Navel Stone.

The New Team

We had to decide on our team before we could do anything. Unlike the previous year, it seemed obvious who should be included this time and there was general agreement that the numbers should be kept low. Even so, we felt new blood was needed to give renewed impetus to the project.

Since the end of the last rendezvous Quenton had moved to Anglesey and we had fallen out of regular contact with Carole and Diana. On the other hand, we had strengthened our friendship with some of the people from the East Midlands branch of the Centre for Crop Circle Studies, in particular with one of their leading members, Karen Douglas. She had simultaneously witnessed the same two bright lights I had seen from Burgess Hill the year before (and would go on to become one of the most active national circle researchers). The East Midlands group had been carrying out similar communication work to us, albeit without psychics and more of a slant toward the extra-terrestrial connection, and it made sense to join forces in 1994. We invited Karen and her colleague Mark Haywood to take part on 28th June, although in the event only Karen would be able to make it.

Despite Paul's experience in the art, we felt we needed another good dowser to determine the exact position of the Navel Stone. As David Russell had already helped us in the past and was familiar to everyone, he was the logical choice for this 'position' and humbly accepted the invitation. After reluctantly leaving Michael Green out of the second two rendezvous attempts, we felt it was only right, given his role in setting all of this up and his experience with ritual and channelling, that he should resume his place. With these new members and reinstatements, together with the original crew of Paul, Barry, Linda, Martin and myself, the Cissbury team was complete.

A preparatory gathering was called at Paul's house for Sunday 13th February. This year, with the importance of attendance stressed, all but David (who was away) managed to reach the meeting, despite some heavy snow - although I nearly didn't. On the Friday my son Jordan was unexpectedly born several weeks early, with a few complications, to my wife Kaye. Karen and Mark were staying the weekend for the meeting and I was glad of the company, cut off from my family left at the hospital. Still, with Jordan now comfortable in the incubator that would be his home for several weeks (he would be fine) and Kaye recovering in a ward, I could see no reason not to abscond for a couple of hours to speak with discarnate entities at Lancing.

At the gathering, we talked with Joeb and Emun and put together our strategy. Most importantly of all, the meeting established that everyone felt comfortable with each other, without the personal uncertainties that had marred the previous year's arrangements. We were ready to move forward.

Reconnaissance

Immediately after the meeting of 13th February, Michael decided he wanted to visit Cissbury for himself and a number of us foolhardily set off for the top of the Ring in the

The summit of Cissbury Ring, at the very site where we would gather on 28th June 1994.

clear but freezing late afternoon. Michael did an initial dowse in the general area where Paul had indicated the Navel Stone once was. After twenty minutes, blue with cold from a biting wind, we were ready to come down and decided that any lengthier investigations would be done in the warmer months! Nevertheless, to have visited the actual place (many of us, incredibly, had never been to the top of Cissbury) where we knew we had to gather later in the year did make the project more real for us and we could visualise the terrain and conditions we might have to face more clearly, although in the event the temperature, at least, would be the extreme opposite of this day.

A few months later, in early May, David, Barry, Martin and myself returned to Cissbury Ring to pin-point more accurately the position of the etheric stone, where we would have to sit on 28th June. In prophetically bright sunshine, David located the spot and marked it with a tiny metal peg and a ribbon which we hoped would remain there until the following month. We photographed the area in case they should be taken away.

Now there was only one task remaining before the big day; to contact Emun's neighbouring Guardians to see if they could help channel energy to Cissbury for our 'higher communication'.

Cened, The Rightful Warrior

One afternoon in mid-May, Paul drove out to the gravel car park of St Mary's at Sompting to see if he could tune in to the Guardian of this important area for crop formations.

The church had long held an air of mystique about it, partly because of its rare architecture (the Saxon spire is virtually unique) and those who used it. Adopted in the middle of the 12th Century by the order of the Knights Templar, some of their myths and associations surrounded the church still. The Templars rose to prominence with the

Carving of interlaced wheat inside St Mary's.

The blocked North Door at St Mary's betrays the church's origins as a Knights Templar 'safe house'.

Crusades and were reputedly revered - and feared - for their understanding of ancient wisdoms. Accusations of the use of occult sorcery and fears that their influence was becoming too strong finally led the order to be forcibly dissolved by the Church in 1312. Even so, initiates managed to continue their practices for a while longer by building secret Templar symbolism into certain churches so that sympathisers would recognise these places as 'safe houses'. One of these symbols formed part of a sculpture which once adorned the front of St Mary's but which was now inside, showing a bull, a lion, an eagle and an angel surrounding Jesus. This sculpture had symbolic connections to the pictogram but two fields away which had triggered our communications with Joeb in 1992. Also inside was a wall frieze depicting interlaced stalks of wheat... Another sign of Templar activity could be seen by the fact that St Mary's had an old blocked door to the north. Templars would always enter a church by the North Door as a sign to others of their faith that they were kindred. The Church finally sussed this and ordered such North Doors to be bricked up. That such a mysterious building was at the centre of an area with so many crop circles seemed appropriate.

Paul discovered that the Guardian of St Mary's was a being named 'Cened' (pronounced *Sened*) - *"The Rightful Warrior,"* as he described himself. Apparently celtic in origin and 'appearance' (such entities seem to retain the image of their last earthly forms, at least when dealing with human channellers), Cened was a gruff-sounding character, fiercely protecting his territory from negative influences.

On 29th May, most of the team set out to speak with Cened themselves. Using as our tuning in point a grassy part of the car-park opened specially for a wedding currently taking place at the church, we were very wary that the vicar or the happy couple's families might descend, accusing us of conducting satanic rituals or something on holy ground! In the event, Paul sat in his car with the door open while we grouped casually on the grass. We probably passed as picnickers unless anyone got close enough to hear Cened's growling tones coming from Paul's mouth...

Cened confirmed what we already knew from Emun and from Paul's earlier conversation with 'The Rightful Warrior', that he could not influence the circle-making forces in any way except by maintaining the energy lines. Similarly, this would be all he could offer for the 28th June:

"I keep the energy lines clear, that is the job of Guardians. That is, they must not be polluted. To make these circles appear, I must make sure I do my job properly, and that is to keep them clear. I have nothing else to do with the formations but I am aware that they need clear energy to get the right result. ...They were attracted to this area because it is necessary for the energy that I look after to be spread and Man to be purified for the people in this area. That is why those particular designs were put down: because they give out a certain balance of energy."

When asked how important St Mary's church was to the area, Cened replied:

"Very important indeed. All of these places that are of the Power are important to the community. But this has been lost and that is why it is so important now that they should be rediscovered. That is why people have come here to worship for so many, many years. It goes back a long time and the energy here spreads out, and the giving of their hearts to God spreads throughout my lines and the lines of the Earth Mother, and the result is the upliftment of Mankind and consciousness here that has been lost. That is why I am so happy to still serve here. ...The people who are coming to this church now do not necessarily seek Christian truths. They seek something else. I am here to help them open up this area."

Curiously, Cened claimed to have no knowledge of the Cissbury Guardians besides being aware of them, and they never conversed. Similarly, Emun had been unable to name any cohorts outside the Ring. Instead, Cened reserved his only contact with another Guardian for the presence he described as "the lady on the hill", a being whose adjoining territory centred on Lancing College chapel, the famous ecclesiastical landmark which overlooked the River Adur in another area of crop circle activity. Cened seemed to have an affectionate respect for this apparently female entity. Paul saw the name 'Armis' for her. It seemed logical that the 'lady on the hill' should be our next port of call. Wisely managing to leave St Mary's before the wedding congregation emerged, we set out in our convoy of cars for Lancing College.

The huge edifice of Lancing College Chapel, focal point for the being we came to know as 'Armis'.

Armis, The Lady On The Hill

We weren't entirely sure if we had to ask permission to enter the grounds of the college but we boldly drove up the long entrance road which led to the huge chapel. If anyone challenged us we would think of something to say or simply leave if we had to.

Parked under a line of leafy trees for shade on this warm afternoon, once again Paul stayed in his motor to see if he could find Armis, while we gathered around. We had never heard Paul channel a female presence before but after a while a soft, very feminine voice began to speak. Armis told us that she had originally come from Greece and retained parts of that persona but that she was more "etheric" than some Guardians and therefore more vulnerable; Cened acted as her protector:

"Even though I have an almost human form it is not as human a form as Cened. Cened is a little more solid and therefore he is, in a sense, more capable of protection. I am more ethereal. ...Cened is my protector. I do work with him but it is mainly if I am being challenged,

which happens. That is the reason why the Earth has Guardians. They can be challenged sometimes when light is pouring through and sometimes it is necessary for him to come and help... But it is not war as you know it."

Armis described her exact role in using Lancing College as her centre:

"This is an area of education, an area of light. This is an area where groups of people, young people, are drawn together for knowledge. I am concerned with keeping up the energies of education, and the education comes from a long way away. I am a small part in the structure of energy and intelligence that comes from afar. This structure of teaching encircles the whole of the world. I have my portion. I keep it pure as best I can. ...There are entities who would disrupt the education programme. There are those who would not let human beings go forward in the light of knowledge, not just in the spiritual sense but also in the sense of the arts. They would disrupt this if they could. This does not happen very often but when it does then I call for Cened and he comes and we drive them off. So far we have been successful."

Armis seemed to take much pride in her work and told us of her great affection for the youths studying at the college, several groups of whom walked past our cars while she was speaking. No-one seemed to bat an eyelid at our presence! Finally, we asked Armis for her advice on our forthcoming expedition to Cissbury Ring. Her answer was simple and direct:

"Approach it with light and love in your heart. You wish to learn. I am part of the education process. You are going there with an open heart to receive enlightenment. Go there with joy. Do not go there with doubt, go with joy always, sit and be quiet and open up to the higher energies as I do. That is all. There is no more for you to know."

There seemed no purpose in disturbing this delightful, warm presence any further and, indeed, we felt that our task in contacting Guardians in advance of the 28th June was complete. Still uncertain as to what would occur on that date, there was little to do now but wait for the big day...

High and exposed, Cissbury Ring, site of our gathering on one of the hottest days of 1994. Photo: John Holloway.

8: TRANSMISSION FROM SIRIUS

Hot Stuff

Karen arrived at my home in Lewes on Monday 27th June to stay over for the main event on the Tuesday. She had been travelling in Wiltshire to look at the many huge and beautiful crop formations which were gracing that part of the countryside and Steve Alexander drove her over. He stayed for a while as we searched for a small pictogram which had been sighted in the Falmer area just outside Brighton and then reluctantly left, agreeing to return the next morning to examine some very strange formations which had appeared at Birling Gap, near Eastbourne. Karen seemed distant and dreamy. It was clear she and Steve were falling in love. After more fruitless searching for the elusive pictogram (which would be discovered eventually) the two of us retired to a Falmer pub and sat outside in the scarlet sunset. The evening was very warm and calm, a pointer to the weather we would experience the following day. We spoke of love, life and crop circles - and of what we should expect from our appointment at Cissbury now only a few hours away...

The 28th June dawned bright and cloudless, conditions which would endure for what would turn out to be one of the very hottest days of 1994. Karen and I set off to meet with Barry, Martin and Michael at the Birling Gap formations, notable - and controversial - because all the crop had been laid down from *halfway up the stems*. A group of international researchers were coming down to view the formations for themselves and we had agreed to meet them there before leaving for Cissbury Ring. Steve arrived with his camera and steel poles for overhead shots but it was clear he was really here for Karen. With our viewing done and the clocks ticking towards our appointment in the car park at the foot of the Ring, we had to drag Karen away for more celestial matters...

Good Golly Miss Molly

Paul made his own way over to Cissbury and tried to compose himself for what was going to be a major test of his stamina and psychic abilities. With no other clairvoyants among the team this year a lot was hanging on his performance. Paul explains:

"It was a day of pre-polio bliss. A golden day that called to me through time when, as a child of six, the sea was my god and sunshine the glow that drove me to mighty adventures that only a child could know. The only difference between that sublime state and here was that I was now an adult, an adult that had programmed himself to worry about a future he couldn't see. As a child there is no fear of the day, only excitement at what is and the acceptance of the gift of the day without thought of the morrow, just the sheer joy of being alive."

"I had reason for being cautious and slightly uneasy. I was being followed, spied on, probed. I cannot say that I was afraid because I was not. There WAS nothing to fear. But I resented this intrusion before the 'event' at Cissbury. I knew that if I tuned in, certain information would follow and I didn't want that; I didn't want to know anything before the appointed hour when I would sit before the site of the Navel Stone and open myself up to God knows what. What the hell had I let myself in for? I was a poet, a writer, a performer of the spoken word; I felt like I was going on stage without learning my lines (every actor's nightmare). But this was nothing new. Joeb did this with me all the time, I never knew exactly what he was going to say next. Why was this different? It *was* different. But I didn't know why and I didn't *want* to know why."

"I was on my own this time. No other psychic back-up from my fellows. If nothing happened that would be it, I would pack up my psychic ability and put it away somewhere to gather dust. I WAS ON MY OWN and it scared me. Yes, I was, after all, a little scared - of failure. Yet despite this feeling, there was some element that told me "everything will be alright. You're doing this for the right reasons, for the pursuit of knowledge, for the eternal quest for truth".

"As I drove to Cissbury Ring I reached to put on a cassette of Albinoni. This beautiful music lifted me to the sky. I stopped. I didn't need lifting, I needed nailing down!"

"I arrived at the old hill-fort with Little Richard belting out *Tutti Frutti* and *Good Golly Miss Molly*. Now I was ready!"

Pitching Camp

At 1.00pm we all gathered at the car park to the north-east of Cissbury Ring and ensconced Paul into the wheelchair, his vehicle for the journey up the hill. No stretchers this year - thank God! The footpaths were bone dry and easy to navigate as Barry and Martin took charge of the pushing duties. With the sun beating down from a sky of glowing blue, we made our way up to the site of the Navel stone and 'pitched camp'.

Amazingly, the little metal peg we had used to mark the spot of the stone was still there. Paul had

Left: *David, Andy, Karen and Paul contemplate final arrangements before settling down to wait for a 'higher communication'. Photo: Barry Reynolds*
Below: *The whole group at the site of the Navel Stone. Photo: Barry Reynolds*

brought a stake of wood to drive into the ground at the site of the missing sarsen and tied an amethyst crystal to the top. Four other crystals were placed on the cardinal compass points around the area where we would sit. Paul explains why:

"In order for me to tune in accurately to the etheric remnants of the Navel Stone I had originally used the dowsing technique of asking the Universal Overself to bring the stone, in its entirety, and place it in the middle of my upper room at the house of saucers. In this way I was able to measure, using dowsing rods, its height and breadth and also, and most importantly, the position of the 'fifth band', the chakric energy band of communication. When I had established this I procured a wooden pole: I measured about six inches up from its base. This was sufficient to push into the ground on the exact position of the original stone once we were at Cissbury itself. From that point up I could measure exactly on the pole where the fifth chakric band would be. Thus done, I cut the pole at that point and secured an amethyst crystal to it with twine."

"The idea of positioning four other crystals around the site was to create a 'Medicine Wheel', a power base of balance. In a sense it was like a psychic Faraday Cage. It created a cocoon of protection. From what I didn't know. But we wanted to create conditions as perfect as perfect could be."

Barry places a stake to mark the missing Navel Stone around which we would all sit. (Video image)

We had been told by Emun to be ready for action at 2.00pm but by 1.45pm Michael still hadn't arrived! We had left him at Birling Gap expecting him to follow soon after. We decided there was nothing we could do but set up to be ready to go ahead if he didn't show.

With Paul facing directly north, wooden stake in front, the six of us, Barry, David, Karen, Linda, Martin and myself, sat in a ring facing inwards about seven feet away from him, leaving a space for Michael in the hope he would eventually arrive. Soon after, with only five minutes to go, he did. His wife Christine, who had driven him down to Sussex from London, had felt ill after leaving the Birling Gap formations, hence the delay. Settling quickly, we began to quieten, taking our shoes and socks off to feel the grass and earth under our feet which we felt gave us more of a connection to the planet beneath - and cooled us off somewhat from the stifling heat which was roasting our skin as we sat.

Paul, rather obscenely ensconced with the stake between his knees, begins to tune in. To what, we had no idea. Photo: Barry Reynolds

We were slightly concerned that the sight of seven barefooted people gathered in a circle around a wheelchair-bound figure holding a wooden pole might draw unwanted attention. After all, Cissbury was a major picnicking and dog-walking spot. And yet, for all the time we sat that afternoon, not a single soul came up to the Ring. We were alone. Perhaps the three Guardians had chased visitors away.

At 2.15pm I activated the video camera which I had brought to record whatever was about to befall and we waited, eager to know what the 'higher communication' would be and anxious for the information which would enable us to finally achieve our aim of filming the crop circle makers in action. At last we would be able to show the world that something massive and incredible was happening. Everyone would have to take notice. Definitely.

Jeuz - The Sermon On The Mount

With one hand on the wooden stake and another clasping the crystal on top, Paul began with an invocation and psychically opened himself up, ready to receive... something:

"Michael placed a small cassette recorder on my lap as I was positioned before the pole and Andy was ready with the video camera nearby. Everyone was strangely quiet, almost respectful as if we were quietly going about our business in some sort of temple. No echoes up here, only the sound of the wind, the cry of gulls and other birds and insects. I faced north with the sea, my beloved sea, at my back but it lay south and that would never do. North was the place of balance; I *had* to face north. I was beginning to tingle. I started the invocation, thanking Emun, Tryst and Rachael for all their work. We had all brought stalks of corn from known crop circles as a gift, a gesture, and perhaps a point of reference. The invocation at an end, I placed my right hand on top of the raised crystal. Almost immediately energy shot through me. I felt it grow stronger, felt the tingling buzz around my head, felt the muscles in my face change, contort into a seeming mask of concrete. With a sudden surge of power the communicant gave his greetings and the message began."

If this experience was to be traumatic and revelatory for Paul, the words which followed, delivered in a dramatic, guttural tone, were profound - and shocking - to we who were awaiting our next instructions as to how to continue our experiments... What follows is a full transcription of the discourse received on top of Cissbury Ring that burning and wonderful afternoon:

"Greetings, greetings. It has been a long time since we have communicated here, a long time.

I understand your frustration concerning the corn circles - but the frustration will continue, because of those who will not accept. You have asked that circles be performed, created; that cannot be tampered with. We have done this, we have done this. But do not think it will be easy for you to use your equipment to film such an event. It is so difficult because of all the various elemental forces necessary to come together for this occasion and to get them to behave. We would like this, but you know - you all know - that 'they' will not believe you even if this were possible. No.

You have to accept that power comes from circles. The reason that they are here is because your Earth now needs to change. The knowledge of this we have known for thousands of years and we have hinted at it through various mediums and channels for so long, so long. DO NOT PLACE SUCH IMPORTANCE ON THE PROOF! You are expanding. All those who are associated with these circles are expanding now and this is only the beginning. You will have

Four frames from the video sequence of the Cissbury communication: ***i)*** *Paul gives the opening invocation, holding a stem from a crop formation.* ***ii)*** *'Jeuz' makes his powerful presence felt and delivers his profound message.* ***iii)*** *Paul pitches forward, his glasses falling to the ground, as Jeuz leaves.* ***iv)*** *Tears, as Paul recovers from the intense experience.*

proof with the corn but who will really believe you? You can turn the world upside down and they will not believe you.

But the spirit of the land rises and blossoms and there will be signs in the sky. You will see this. We hope it will be this year that you will see this. But you will. And they will still not believe. But what does it matter? The circles are here to help with this so-called 'rising of the Earth'. She must rise up now and join us. She is like a child to us in space, a jewel, and she is waiting to flourish, to become who she really is and to take you all with her. It is such a journey - such a fantastic journey! - and you are part of that journey and you must ride with her. You understand what I am saying to you? You must ride with her and keep the love of God, whatever you conceive that energy to be, in your heart and keep it alive - KEEP IT ALIVE! And the beauty will continue. Lights in the sky. More corn circles. But there is only so much that we can do, only so much. You say they are miracles - yes, we ARE miracle workers - but there are limits. We cannot change the mind of Man. He must do that. You, my friends here, all changed to what you were, and it is only the beginning of vast changes.

(Michael: "Friend, who are you?") *"Trying to get a name through this channel... Jeuz. J-E-U-Z. Jeuz. I am not of human form. I am not. But similar, similar. Sirius. Dog Star. Yes."*

(Michael: "What is your role with us who are part of the Ascension process?") *"The influence that we are giving. Beings such as we are surround the Earth, giving inspiration and support to all those who seek the Light. That is our job, yes, that is it. We have been around for a long time, during great civilisations upon this Earth. I am a spokesman. I have not spoken for a long time. I have come to tell you not to place too much importance on trivia, of trying to prove this or that. It is happening, yes it is happening and will continue."*

"Energy going now. Energy going now."

(Michael: "Thank you for coming to speak with us.") *"It is my pleasure. To all of you here - ALL of you here - blessings from us. From us we send you our love. Please continue to work in the Light. Please do this, not for yourself but for the whole of the Earth for she is beautiful, far more beautiful than you will know. But given time you will know how beautiful she is. Continue with your work, but do not be bogged down by trying to prove this or that because in the end IT MAKES NO DIFFERENCE - none! Bless you. Thank you."*

With that, 'Jeuz' was gone. The spiritual vacuum left by his departure had Paul pitching forward in his chair. His sunglasses fell to the ground. Suddenly he was sobbing, not with joy or sorrow but with a sense of release. We sat in silence, stunned by Jeuz's words and by the curiously affecting sight of our friend's outpouring. There was a stillness in the air and the world seemed to stop for a few minutes, Paul's weeping and distant birdsong the only sound. He recalls how he felt:

"When Jeuz left me my breathing was short and laboured and I was feeling slightly torn and battered but in the sense that something had been achieved - that was it: a sense of achievement... but I was crying, crying out of me something that I had never experienced before. I was bursting with energy, neither happy nor sad. The only expression I had left were tears and they came thick and hard. I didn't care who saw or who turned away. This was real. I had nothing to prove anymore. The words of Jeuz were not just words of great power but of great wisdom and I was proud to be his spokesman. The tears were a by-product of something much deeper."

"After the tears I shook for about ten minutes. And in all the time we spent at this holy place not a soul came near. Perhaps our psychic Faraday Cage, created by the four cardinal point crystals, was working better than we could ever have imagined."

"I remember someone asking me later whether I would ever channel Jeuz again. I said I didn't know. Certainly not in the immediate future, maybe never. I'd think about it if and when I was asked. All I wanted now was to go home and have a cup of tea. Weeks later I saw the video of the event. I had forgotten so much of what he had said and at the end the tears came again. More gently this time."

The Message Sinks In

We would not consider the words of Jeuz (pronounced *Jee-ooze*) deeply until they had time to sink in properly. Immediately our friend from Sirius left and after Paul had recovered enough to close with a short prayer, we shook ourselves out of the intensity

The Cissbury team (minus Andy, taking the photo), hot and happy after their descent from the Ring, still yet to absorb the full implications of the 'transmission from Sirius'.

of the experience and began to chat quietly. Michael placed an arm around Paul's shoulder. He too had felt the power of Jeuz from where he was sitting and was drained of energy, rather like Barry had been, in the car with Emun when the Guardian first spoke. David, just a little further from Paul, had also felt the same effect, as if he had "A head full of soup". The intense heat didn't help. Karen's very fair skin had turned an alarming shade of red and sunstroke was setting in.

Overall though, we felt happy, cheerfully packed up the equipment and made our way back down the hill. As we spoke about what had transpired, we began to realise that Jeuz had effectively ended the first phase of our communication work - by telling us that our attempts to video a crop circle forming might never be successful and that if they were it wouldn't change the world in the way we thought because those who couldn't accept the authenticity of the phenomenon never would, whatever the evidence.

Other aspects Jeuz had spoken about would be dissected over the weeks, his words about the 'rising of the Earth' and of 'signs in the sky'. Joeb had already talked of 'astrograms' which would be witnessed, elaborate aerial shapes of light which would perform a similar function to the crop circles. Later in the summer a number of reports from around the country were recorded of complex 'paper doilies' seen forming in the sky and Linda would observe yet another strange glowing object over the Reynolds household.

As we retired to Paul's house for tea, our euphoria at having contacted the higher realms we had aspired to waned a little as we began to realise the true implications of the message. On one level we had been given inspiration and a pat on the back, but on another we had received a ticking off for having spent so much time trying to achieve something we didn't really need. We had all seen enough to know that the crop circle phenomenon was real and beyond the capability of human hoaxers in most cases, whatever anyone else thought. What were we trying to prove to ourselves? Those outside the immediate influence of the circles themselves might be swayed by a video of one appearing but many of those we were trying to convince would never have their minds changed, no matter how remarkable the proof. Jeuz had tried to make us see that it didn't really matter what others thought. The crop circles were carrying out their task regardless, affecting the people they needed to reach. Scepticism from some couldn't change or devalue the real task of the formations, which, from what the 'transmission from Sirius' had implied, seemed to be as Joeb had told us from the beginning.

Yet with the feeling of disappointment which derived from not having been given the information we had expected came a sort of relief. At last we could lose the intense *need* for proof we had craved. Suddenly, it was as if we had been given permission simply to run and play with the crop circles, relax and enjoy ourselves without having to force anyone's view to our own. From this time on, an ease would set in with some of the team which would actually enable us to tell others about the circles phenomenon with a greater clarity and objectivity far more attractive and interesting to those new to the crop patterns than any of the coercive approaches we might have displayed before. Consequently, we probably turned *more* people onto them because we didn't feel we had anything to prove!

With these thoughts in our heads we returned to our homes somehow happier for the experience of the day. Karen was out for the count though. Lovesick and sunstroked, she fell asleep on our sofa mid-evening. I placed a duvet cover over her and shut the living room door. Next day I would return her to Steve and a partnership which would flourish romantically - and spread knowledge of the crop formations yet further - was born.

More About Jeuz

In the weeks that followed, Paul received a number of insights into Jeuz and learnt more about our apparent communicant from the Dog Star:

"I had no vision about Jeuz but I did have a 'knowing'. A 'knowing' is a kind of clairvoyance in that when one gets this feeling of 'exactness' one just *knows* that the information is correct, and I've proved this to myself time and time again. My feeling about Jeuz was that he was a Lion Person, a 'Paschat' as some call them, from the star system of Sirius, the Dog Star, which clairvoyants had visualised as being tall leonine humanoids. I phoned my friend, the writer and expert on Egyptian magic, Murry Hope. I asked her whether the name 'Jeuz' seemed right for a being from Sirius. Her answer was yes, the frequency of the name seemed perfectly right to her. Murry had received much psychic information from the Lion People and she felt a close affinity with this advanced race of beings. I told her of our communication and she didn't seem at all surprised."

Sirius has long had influence over humankind's development, whether symbolically or genuinely. Ancient Egypt held the star as sacred, equating it with the Goddess Isis, and the African Dogon tribe believe that their race originated from a planet in the Sirian star system. Curiously, they have long had records of astronomical details about that system that modern science is only now establishing for itself. (In 1995 a small but intricate formation was found etched into forest floor materials at Kingley Vale, West Sussex - this bore a resemblance to an old Dogon symbol representing the descent of the 'Nommos' ship which they believe brought their race to Earth.)

One aspect that almost got overlooked from the Cissbury communication was that it seemed we had finally managed to speak directly to one of the forces responsible for creating the circles. Taken at face value "***We** are miracle workers*" certainly appeared to suggest that Jeuz was claiming his race was part of the 'space people' which Joeb had referred to, working in association with the Devic forces and the Earth Mother to create the crop patterns. All along, our experiment had taken the stance of accepting the channelled messages for what they appeared to be, whatever the personal opinions of individual group members, and on this level at least, we could claim to have finally reached out and spoken with the circle-makers themselves. It took a while to grasp the significance of this. Paul agrees:

"Andy and I spoke of Jeuz in the years after and we both recorded a sense of having not quite 'appreciated the moment' or the importance of his words at the time and the love and power therein. It was only later on that we began to realise how great a moment it was atop Cissbury Ring."

In the months that followed, Paul's poetic nature gave inspirational birth to the following words for Jeuz, included in his poetry compendium *The Drunk on the Train* (see appendices):

Help me to
Understand, Jeuz?

I tampered
And stroked
The crystal
(Raised to communication level)
Set on the ancient site
Of men far wiser
Than I.

And you screamed
Your message
Through me
From a distant star.

When you were done,
Your message spent
I wept out
Your spent energy,
Neither in joy
Or pain.

But now I feel
Your loss.
Though you followed me
Like a spy
During the interim
Of our union,
Setting my emotions
In concrete clay:
A holy preparation
For the speak.
I was still torn,
Maybe changed.

Do you really
Have the courage
Of the lion
That I saw,
Will I share again
That joyous energy?

I grasped
Time and Space
In my hands
And expressed it
The only way I could…
With tears.

Project Sky

In addition to her involvement with the team's communication work, Karen had been instrumental in setting up what became known as (aptly, as it turned out) '*Project Sky*', an attempt to unite scattered groups of crop circle enthusiasts by getting them to meditate outside at specific sites across the country simultaneously.

On 1st July, just three days after Jeuz had graced us with his presence, Barry and I, together with about twelve other CCCS Sussex members, returned to the top of Cissbury Ring to take part in *Project Sky*. There seemed no better place to congregate than once again around the site of the Navel Stone, although only Barry and myself knew what had transpired on that spot previously.

While Karen's team gathered up in the East Midlands and other groups did the same around England, we settled down peacefully at the agreed time of 9.00pm as the weather grew turbulent over the oceans around the coast, visible from our vantage point high up on the Ring. A storm was preparing. There was a magical feeling to the evening, the sky a restless tumble of purple and red clouds circling around Cissbury, a calm at the centre.

As we sat, our minds in free-fall, we became aware of the shifting moods of the weather. A light shower passed briefly. Warm breezes rose and fell, followed by colder

Lightning tears the air at Cissbury, the night of Project Sky. *(Video image)*

currents. Lightning began to flicker out to sea. It was as if we were feeling the living breath of the planet in motion, halting our usual ceaseless activities just long enough to acknowledge and feel the ever-changing bio-mechanisms of the Earth at work.

As the evening progressed the storm grew wilder and more violent. And yet it seemed to take place around us, never threatening the Ring itself. Perhaps the topography of the ancient hill-fort and the surrounding downs drove the storm into a vortex which left Cissbury untouched. Or perhaps the three Guardians were protecting us. At least two of our number sensed a presence among us as we sat quietly. By chance, if chance it was, Karen's group was experiencing almost exactly the same weather conditions. They also found themselves surrounded by lightning but remained untouched by the storm.

An enduring memory of that night was of one of our members standing, arms outstretched to the sky, silhouetted against the lightning-illuminated clouds, a human being at the mercy of, and yet somehow in harmony with, the elemental forces.

We had come up here to acknowledge the circle-making forces, as a kind of gesture of response just to say "We're here. What do you want us to do next?". Making a little closing invocation, I asked the circle-making forces to respond in whatever way they felt most appropriate. Almost immediately, a huge scarlet-tinged bolt of lightning tore through the air overhead. It was time to leave. Up here, high and exposed, we couldn't rely on the Ring to protect us indefinitely. We made our way down to the cars and said our farewells.

Linda's Light

As the violent wonders of nature were encircling us at Cissbury, Linda Reynolds, who had been unable to find a child-minder for her and Barry's two sons, sat just inside her open patio doors at Burgess Hill, tuning in for *Project Sky* while facing the garden from which so many strange sightings had been made the year before.

At about 9.15pm she felt compelled to open her eyes - which immediately alighted on a very bright object hanging low in the sky ahead. It couldn't be a star; there was a heavy and turbulent cloudbase as far as the eye could see, preparing for the storm whose birth we were witnessing at Cissbury. The object began to approach then turned a narrow anticlockwise circle to the north. Used to aeroplanes and helicopters flying low into Gatwick airport a few miles away, Linda was sure this was neither of these.

Suddenly the light vanished - but something was still visible as a dark shadow moving in front of the orange-glowing clouds, illuminated by the lamps of the town. If the light hadn't gone out then the object had rotated so the glow was no longer visible. With the brightness extinguished, Linda could see its shape. It appeared to be rectangular with rounded ends. A domed bulge emanated from the underside. Turning another anticlockwise circle, it travelled across the sky again and was lost from view to the north-west.

Shaken by this experience, her heart pumping vigorously, Linda moved back into the house. In one of the rooms were bundles of barley stems which had been taken from the Birling Gap crop formations earlier in the week, to send for analysis by Dr Levengood, a scientist in America who was studying circle-affected crop. Compelled to move towards the drying samples, Linda found herself standing over a specific batch. Suddenly she felt a "terrible feeling of pins and needles and crackles," going up and down her right arm as she held it over one of the samples. Fascinated but perturbed by this, the feeling grew very uncomfortable and she had to walk away.

Once again, Barry and Linda's house had become a focus for strange happenings during the course of the communication experiments.

Which Way Now?

I wasn't ready to go home after leaving Cissbury Ring the night of *Project Sky*. I needed to think. I drove down to the coast, parked up in Paul's road and walked to the quiet seafront nearby. The storm was dying now, moving back out to sea. Distant lightning danced in strange patterns out over the dark water, the thunder almost inaudible. Sipping coffee from a flask, I began to get recent events in perspective.

For two years now we had tried to interact with the circle-making forces. We had lived through some fascinating experiences but still didn't have the crowning glory to round off our work, something to show for our efforts that could be presented to the outside world without any ambiguity. Jeuz had pointed out the folly of trying to prove things to those who would never listen and his message made sense. Yet our work didn't feel as if it was over. There was more we had to do, perhaps one final stage we had to take it to. But what?

Our original plan had been, once we had the secret knowledge we needed from the 'higher source' Emun had promised us, to try another rendezvous like the previous year's before the summer of 1994 ended. But the apparent Sirian communication seemed to stall that. Jeuz had told us there could be no guarantees the experiment would ever be a success. If it was, would it convince those we were trying to reach anyway? With the wind taken out of our sails somewhat in that direction and a kind of calmer equilibrium reached in our minds as to how we should continue our research, we all felt the work for this season was done.

We would have to consider carefully what to do next year. As 1994 passed, our thoughts turned to ways of providing ourselves with a grand finale.

Wolstonbury Hill, another Iron Age hill-fort crafted from the South Downs. The ring of the summit can be seen at the top left of the picture. For 1995's experiment, we would sit just to the right of this, close to the path. Photo: John Holloway

9: THE WOLSTONBURY EXPERIMENT

Fresh Pastures

In the wake of the Jeuz communication, all thoughts of conducting another rendezvous on the same lines as before had deserted. But some aspects of the work - the apparent interactive events which had created a formation for the meeting held at Paul's house and mutated another on the first night out, the shared vision of the three psychics in 1993 and the apparent stimulation of unusual light/object phenomena - had suggested that we were touching on *something* tangible worth persevering with. All this appeared to be generated in proportion to the intensity of our own activities.

It began to dawn on us that perhaps we should capitalise on this observation. All of our communication experiments had fundamentally revolved around hungrily waiting, expecting, looking for something to deliver the goods to *us*, with little or no return from ourselves besides our physical efforts to be present. Maybe the deal was too one-sided. It was time for us to give something back. Little did we know how successful this change of emphasis would prove to be.

We, The Circle-Makers

If we were going to continue our work in 1995, we would have to take a new direction. Paul believed he had one. He had long believed that some of the crop patterns were already present within the Earth's energy grid on an 'etheric' level. In other words, a junction point which could take on a particular shape with the right impetus was already present as an energy field but needed to be triggered in some way to physically exist as a trace mark in a crop field. Paul began to form a plan whereby the group itself would attempt to 'light the blue touch paper' on one of these etheric energy fields:

"Almost from the beginning of my association with 'croppies' and crop circles I had held the theory that many of the glyphs in the corn were *already there!* Etheric geometric patterns of power. This was based on the idea that places like Stonehenge and Avebury had existing webs of energy that were enhanced by the placing of sarsens, amplified by the crystalline structure of the stones. The stone complexes themselves, as physical representatives of the etheric pattern, were connected by earth energy lines to power sites in the area. This energy was heightened by the position of the sun and moon, planets and stars and was in some way connected to the Universe, all of it a kind of mechanism for communication."

"Therefore it seemed to me that if I could find a suitable site where an existing etheric energy pattern was, by activating its connecting power line by whatever means, we might, just *might,* be able to bring a crop down ON that spot. The idea was wild but what had we to lose but a bit of face?"

There had been one or two recorded instances of groups meditating on particular shapes only to find them soon after as crop formations. The American extra-terrestrial investigation team CSETI had visualised a design through meditation in 1992 which, the same night, turned up in a field at Oliver's Castle, Wiltshire. We ourselves had attempted something similar at the CCCS branch meetings in 1993 and the triangular triplet had subsequently born a resemblance to our chosen shape - which by synchronistic chance was almost identical to CSETI's. In these cases either existing etheric power points were being influenced by thought to take on specific forms or maybe our minds were simply picking up on configurations already present in the local energy grid and we weren't inventing our chosen shapes at all.

Perhaps on these occasions the power of thought was flowing down the Earth's energy lines and providing the ignition to kick a junction point into our physical dimension as a crop design. Though this didn't necessarily mean all crop formations were created in this way (some seemed too elaborate and specific), at the very least it showed that the human mind seemed to be a link in the chain of whatever was creating the circles, a combination of extra-terrestrial intelligence, Devas and the Earth Spirit according to Joeb. It was time to put this to the test, without ambiguity. We would track down one of these etheric circuits and try to bring it into our dimension by pouring mind energy into the Earth. We ourselves would become the circle-makers.

This time, however, we would remove some of the pressure for success. Although we planned to film our chosen field while we conducted the experiment, we wouldn't necessarily expect anything to happen at that very moment. If a crop formation were to appear at the designated site any time that summer, or indeed in seasons after, this would be an achievement in itself as we didn't know how long it would take the energy grid to respond to our input. Not long as it turned out...

Wolstonbury Hill as seen from nearby Hurstpierpoint.

Wolstonbury Hill

It wasn't always an exact science but dowsing had served us well in finding our original rendezvous spot and the site of the Navel Stone at Cissbury. It was time to get the maps and pendulums out to locate the site of an etheric energy pattern.

Paul soon identified one. By chance or otherwise, it was at Saddlescombe, just quarter of a mile north and across the other side of the road from where we had conducted our first two rendezvous nights in 1993. Over the hill was Pyecombe which had been visited by two crop formations in previous years. We would discover that at the site was - usefully! - a wheat field, gently sloping down towards a farm in a narrow valley. The energy line which passed through the field seemed to come from Wolstonbury Hill, another ancient hill-fort a couple of miles north-east. Recent archaeological digs had unearthed evidence suggesting that this downland promontory had been shaped as a henge in Neolithic times. Barry had watched his light traversing the A23 from its lower slopes two years previously. The signs were good. Paul describes his discovery of the site:

"I had known for many years, even before I came to Sussex from Kent, that Wolstonbury Hill was a real 'Place of Power'. Colin Bloy, master dowser and healer, had spent time at this wonderful place with his children many years before and found patterns of existing energy in the terrain. But more than that, my psychic 'nose' told me that this was where I should look, in and around Wolstonbury."

"Placing my Ordnance Survey map of the Wolstonbury area on my breakfast-bar I started to section off places surrounding this place of power. I whittled it down to an area around Saddlescombe. Using my pendulum and a pencil as a pointer I whittled down yet again until it whirled its approval and I found a spot which told me that not only was this a powerful place but that it had an existing etheric pattern already established. It was connected by an energy line to Wolstonbury Hill. Coincidentally, this line also ran on to a pre-reformation church near Shoreham-by-Sea and went right through the old lighthouse at Shoreham harbour. Where human beings are active, either verbally or in action concerning the welfare of their souls, then these places are connected to the earth energy grid."

"David confirmed my findings: "A powerful place, Paul," he said to me. But how to activate this pattern in the young corn? I knew from experience that to channel light and power into something one must use the 'place of the Will' ie. the solar plexus. When my meditation groups sent golden light to help Ayesha, the Earth Mother, we funnelled light out of our solar plexus and into the heart of Ayesha. This was the method we would use to energise our chosen location."

However, we would not sit at Saddlescombe to conduct our experiment but at Wolstonbury Hill, the source of the etheric pattern's umbilical energy line. Here we would feed our thought power into the line, telegraphing it to its destination from afar. To input at the source made sense but also, by removing ourselves from the site of where we expected the circle itself to appear and instead sitting where the actual creative energy was being generated, we would be more relaxed and undistracted from the task in hand. If at the field itself, we would be constantly roving with our eyes, waiting for something to happen, like our original rendezvous. This time we would be able to put our egos and immediate wishes to one side to concentrate on simply channelling energy into the ground. A video camera would be at Saddlescombe anyway, should something happen instantaneously.

Welcome Aboard

A new team member came aboard for this experiment, to join our existing crew. Jason Porthouse, a leather-clad biker whose initial appearance belied a gentle, spiritual nature, had been growing progressively closer to the group since being present at the very first appearance of Joeb on that stormy night. He and his brother Mark had seemingly invoked the arrival of the Sompting pictogram of 1992. That event had started all this off. It seemed appropriate that Jason should join us for this phase of the work, which sought specifically to achieve a similar response.

Damus

The Guardians of Cissbury had been instrumental in setting up our meeting with Jeuz. Although our approach was rather different this year, it seemed sensible and courteous to consult the Guardian of the area we would be working in. One day in February, Paul and Jason explored to find the exact location of the field and to contact the resident spirit of Wolstonbury:

"Jason and I set out for Wolstonbury Hill. Apart from its known mystical context it was also a very beautiful place. We drove to the bottom of the hill, deciding to try and make contact with the Guardian without leaving the car. After all, Emun had come through without a hitch at Cissbury Ring and that too was in a vehicle. I suggested to Jason that he also try and open up to any presence. We both sat and tuned-in psychically with a mental request for contact. The Guardian had a couple of goes at 'connecting'. In the end he made it and my face broke out in a huge smile. Jason also felt his smile and it was this that became endemic of the being we came to know and love as 'Damus', Guardian of Wolstonbury Hill."

"Jason questioned Damus and asked him whether he could help in our quest to bring down a crop circle fed by an energy line that came from here. Damus said that he would be delighted! I could feel the joy in him, a child-like joy of someone who had been 'kept in' and was now able to 'go out and play' with human beings, something that he had not done in hundreds of years. He told us that he would help us all he could - but could guarantee nothing! From that moment on, whenever Jason or I went anywhere near Wolstonbury Damus would make a gentle 'grab' at us and we would feel his gentle, childish glee and, above all, his huge grin. God knows what our passengers thought: "What the hell are you smiling about?" they would say. "Oh nothing, just thinking about someone I know."

"Later on, Damus told us that when the wind was in a certain position and force Wolstonbury Hill 'whistled'. Perhaps the original name was the Whistling Hill? He was a Druid and had been chosen to take over from the previous Guardian BEFORE he died in the earthly sense. It was a very great honour and he was delighted to accept. He told us that he had to 'strike the oak' six times to complete his promise that he would serve the area known as Wolstonbury."

Name That Tune

A month or so later, the entire team gathered once again at the house of the saucers to speak with Damus *en masse* and to discuss the project ahead. First of all we needed a date and time. Damus gave us one: We should ascend Wolstonbury Hill and be ready to conduct our meditation on *"The last New Moon in June - at sunset"*. The quickest calculation revealed that we were back to our old friend... the 28th June! Dawn and sunset were powerful times, when the Devic and elemental forces were at their strongest, we were told.

As our intent was to pour as much energy as we could into the line connecting Wolstonbury to Saddlescombe, we needed to know how we might best go about this. How could our thoughts be focused and strengthened to maximum effect? Damus suggested that the use of specific crystals would be beneficial, through which to amplify our mind energy. He also stressed the importance of sound. Damus had already intimated this in an earlier communication with Paul who had subsequently divined that a certain sequence of musical notes would need to be played during our meditation:

"Joeb had said to us so many times through the years: "*Sound is so important. Do you think all the great and not-so-great religions chanted in their different ways for nothing!?*" Damus was no exception to this and when questioned he told us that sound was indeed a vital element. Prior to the meeting, I had dowsed out a chord of music that would, perhaps, resonate with the natural sound that each of the eight sections, or 'Courier lines' (more of which later) of a main earth energy line possessed, ie. the first Courier line was C natural, the second Courier line D natural, the third E natural and so on. The chord I dowsed out was: A, B flat, C sharp, D, F and G sharp."

Joeb had always maintained that sound played a part in the construction of crop formations and Damus' advice seemed to make sense to Paul given what we had been told before:

"An example of sound and geometry is demonstrated by pouring sand onto a cymbal, covering its surface. When the cymbal is struck the sand forms into beautiful patterns. Of course with crop circles the makers were using something more high-tech, well at least by OUR standards they were."

A friend of Paul's recorded the divined notes using an electronic keyboard in bell-like tones. Played individually the sequence had a strange, almost bluesy feel to it. As a chord it gave a discordant but not incoherent effect. The notes were demonstrated to Damus for his approval, which he gave. But everyone agreed the sound wasn't quite right. We would have to listen to it for the duration of our meditation. We needed an audible backdrop that wouldn't disturb our concentration.

Martin, with his musical experience, suggested that if the notes themselves had some kind of useful property to the experiment, which we assumed they must, it would be wise to record them in the purest form available - sine waves. Using a synthesiser, Martin was able to distinguish this distinctive waveform of sound and recorded the notes as a droning chord. The result sounded like a high-pitched whistling or warbling, rather like a fax machine produces when it makes a connection. Curiously, it also sounded uncannily like the controversial 'trilling' noise which has been heard and recorded around crop formations over the years and recalled Vivien and Gary Tomlinson's description of "pan-pipes" as a circle appeared around them. The sine waves didn't sound musical but we instinctively felt this was the right way to take it. An alternative version I produced using an orchestral strings-type sound was rejected after being deemed too much like the score for a horror movie.

Prophetic Doodles

As the notes of music were discussed at the meeting with Damus, Barry's mind began to go into overdrive. He had a intuitive hunch that if a formation was to result from this sequence it would consist simply of "six circular elements", each one a different size, arranged in some kind of configuration though he didn't know what. Although circular shapes sounded like an obvious possibility, by 1995 virtually any pattern could be expected to appear in a field; yet Barry felt instinctively that what we might receive would be simple. Mulling this over, in biro he sketched a single circle above a larger circle with a single standing ring, in turn above a still larger circle with two standing rings. When Damus left and we chatted afterwards, Barry passed the notebook doodle around. We all nodded, said yes, how interesting, and carried on our conversations...

Crystal Tips And Couriers

So far we had used crystals in our work only lightly, first in the kebab formation and then atop Cissbury Ring. This time we felt they should play a greater role, especially as Damus had encouraged their use. Our discovery of 'Courier Lines', information-carrying sub-sections which made up the major energy lines, would shape our work distinctly, as Paul describes:

"Whether we like it or not we are all hooked in to the Earth's energy grid by our own chakric system. As each chakra in the human body has its own colour and sound so then do the Courier lines; the *same* colours the *same* notes of sound. Courier lines are givers and receivers of information just as the human chakric system is. When great music plays, a wonderful orator speaks, a baby cries, or even when politicians babble, all of it is carried by the Courier lines. Every church and temple, hospital and council chamber, every town, every city is connected like some cosmic superhighway, or computer web. Information is stored and given out just like a computer. The level of energy you put in is what you get out. Your body radiates who you are, your character, your YOUness, created by you and your circumstances. So then, a village or town has a character all its own because it radiates who and what it is, and it is human beings that make it what it is! If a foul deed has been done at some place, the Courier lines carry and give out that feeling of negativity and evil. If a place has been given over to tranquillity and peace then that is what you will find. Enter a room after a violent row and you will feel the bad 'vibes'. Of course this will disappear. But if negativity is continued day after day, then it can take years to dispel. What is that shudder you feel when you go near a certain person? You are picking up who he or she really is. The Courier lines do the same job."

"The Courier lines are rising in number globally, the major energy lines continually splitting into finer divisions. The more they multiply the more esoteric information is being poured into the grid from higher sources, information that has been kept from human beings for thousands of years because of fear of misuse by notorious global elites."

"At the time of our experiment at Wolstonbury there was a nine line Courier system - although only eight were fully functional, the energy of the ninth still only rising slowly - and we needed to have crystals that were the same colour and frequency as the human/Earth chakric system. I called Jan Lynch, a healer who uses colour and sound in her work. She was able to advise me as to what crystals were suitable. Once they were collected I dowsed out who would have which, cleansed them and put them away for the big day."

Upward Mobility

There was, of course, the usual challenge presented by having to perform a ritual on top of a hill - getting Paul up there. Wolstonbury Hill wasn't the easiest of sites to ascend. The clearest path to it, which didn't involve steep inclines, was a footpath a quarter of a mile long running from Clayton. This seemed a long way to push a wheelchair and we certainly weren't going back to stretchers!

With this in mind, Jason and I set out one afternoon in May to find a more accessible spot on the lower slopes of Wolstonbury where the group could gather. Wherever it was it would have to be on the energy line which ran from the summit to Saddlescombe as a crucial part of this experiment was to sit on the line itself. Jason pin-pointed some fields behind stables and farmsteads at Pyecombe which ran down from Wolstonbury and overlooked the A23 road. One isolated spot we found would have been ideal were it not for its wheelchair inaccessibility. Only later would we discover that this was the very same field from which Barry had seen the light crossing the dual carriageway two years before... another odd 'coincidence'. Eventually we found the perfect place - a grazing meadow of long grass and wild flowers which could easily be reached via a bridleway. We would be able to drive part of the way and push Paul for the short remainder. The energy line ran directly through the field. Only one problem remained; getting permission from the landowners.

We soon tracked down the stables which owned the field and nervously knocked on the door of the adjoining house. A lady came to the door. We didn't say exactly what we wanted to do but told her we were part of a dowsing group who wanted to conduct a meditation at sunset on 28th June. Surprisingly, she was very open-minded and quite happy for us to go up there. There was only one problem - she would have to check this with her husband. A few days later we got the call. Her husband didn't want any New Age freaks holding occult raves on his land. She was sorry, but we would have to go elsewhere.

There simply wasn't anywhere left for us to try, easy to get to, close to Wolstonbury and on the energy line. There was nothing for it, we would have to wheel Paul all the way to the top of the hill-fort using the Clayton pathway.

The bank overlooking the field at Saddlescombe where we believed our self-triggered crop formation would appear (seen here in winter).

On the same afternoon Jason and I searched Pyecombe, we also made a full reconnaissance of Saddlescombe and walked to the field where we hoped our formation would appear. A public footpath ran along a bank which overlooked it. The farm itself was perilously close and it didn't seem prudent to inform the owners that we were planning to vandalise their field, albeit metaphysically. It was just as well we wouldn't be conducting the actual experiment here. Nevertheless, Steve Alexander had agreed to watch the field for us with a video camera while we meditated at Wolstonbury and he would get a good view from the bank. As he had captured a ball of light on video before, he seemed a good choice for the task. He was disappointed he wouldn't be with Karen and the whole team but in many ways was in a privileged position - if anything *did* transpire that evening he would be the only witness to the creation of the resulting crop circle!

Message From Elle

After an agonising wait, 28th June was almost upon us. It seemed incredible to believe it was exactly a year since our meeting with Jeuz, and two years and a day from our very first rendezvous.

On the evening of the 27th, with only hours to go, Paul received a telephone call which was to alter the nature of our work the next day and placed the final part of a jigsaw which had never seemed quite complete. The caller was Tony Mezen, whose news about the incredible geometric shapes he had seen traversing the sky over his house two years previously had so lifted Paul's spirits in the wake of our first failure. Since his sighting Tony had been developing his own gift for channelling and through this he had received a message for Paul:

"Tony phoned to say that he had received information for me at two o'clock in the morning from a being called 'Elle' (pronounced *Elly*). "Do you know anyone called Elle?" he said. I went on to tell him that 'Elle' or 'Ellen' was one of my favourite names for the Earth Mother, known to many as Gaia and to Joeb as Ayesha. Tony was anxious to tell me the message that he had scribbled down. He read it to me over the phone whilst I wrote his words. The message read:

"*I am your Wyvern. It is the top, not level nor rocky, but earth on top. That is where Elle sleeps. But warning: do not wake Elle without magic iron. Bring song and word. Fire without soot, water without mud. Pure fire. Pure water. Earth and air are as they are. Move where the path leads. Only three. No more. One staff, three stones. Many lie there, with marks, without marks. Between two...*" The message ended abruptly."

"This hit me right in the solar plexus. I knew I had to made sense of it. I felt it must be a reference to the 28th! Tony, again, had no idea of what we were intending, or that we were engaging in any sort of experiment... let alone the next day!"

"I read the message over the phone to Andy. Two weeks before, he had walked to the site at Wolstonbury to check out the terrain for practicalities. I asked whether the description "*It is the top, not level nor rocky, but earth on top*" fitted. He said that it wasn't quite the top but as high as we could sensibly get with a wheelchair. It was indeed 'not level nor rocky'. 'The earth on top' he wasn't sure about. I told him that I was taking this very seriously indeed and felt that when the message said "*Only three. No more*", this referred to Jason, Andy and myself. The "*One staff*" was Damus! (He always carried a staff in my psychic vision, probably the same one with which he struck the oak all those centuries ago). I told Andy not to worry, I'd sort it out. The last thing we all wanted at this late stage was a problem."

"A Wyvern was a mythical and Heraldic animal resembling a dragon. Dragon or Serpent energy was very often used by the ancients to describe earth energy, or *kundalini*. I charged some water by visualising light pouring into the liquid, then, as back-up, I left it in the sun all that day and the next. The reference to "*three stones*" was to my mind objects that we would find on top of the hill but in the event we were never to discover its meaning."

"Meanwhile I got together an agate fire stone to represent the "*Fire without soot*", the fire that does not burn! For the "*iron*" I used a rare iron or bungie stone that had been given to me by Tony many months before. I wrote a separate invocation for the three of us, distinct from the one that I was going to use for the main event. I knew that this small ceremony with the stones and purified water must be performed BEFORE the main invocation and activity of the whole group. In my mind this was what Jason, Andy, myself and Damus were to do. On finding the place (if it existed) where "*Many lie there. With marks, without marks*," Andy would have to sprinkle the now fully charged 'holy' water. To Jason I would give the iron stone and for my part I had the fire stone; these we would have to bury at a given time. What Damus would do I had no idea. What all this was supposed to achieve I had no idea. I felt pretty stupid when asked. I just knew it was right and that some extraordinary alchemical process was going to take place."

The Ninth Band

Wednesday 28th June dawned. When the sun touched the opposite horizon we would have to be ready. But as late as that morning, Jason, who had been appointed the task of dowsing to see who should sit on which part of the energy line, was still having trouble. He was being told that Karen wasn't to sit on any of the eight sections and that Paul - who we had assumed would sit apart from the group - should take her place!

Paul checked Jason's findings and got the same result. We found this hard to believe; after all, Karen had taken part in the Cissbury communication and fitted perfectly into the team. Why this apparent cosmic rebuke?

Jason telephoned me with the problem. As he spoke, the thought struck that as Karen was the newest acquaintance of the team, perhaps she should sit on the newest part of the energy line - the ninth band. It had not occurred to Paul and Jason that this should be used but when the question was put to their pendulums there came a resounding YES. Karen would be responsible for activating the ninth Courier. Paul explains its significance:

"The reason I had decided not to use the number nine Courier was simply that at that point it was only functioning to about 25% of its capacity and it seemed to make sense not to use it. This, as it turned out, was wrong! My 'Earth' logic and 'cosmic' logic don't always mix! Later on I learned that using a Courier line for reasons of humanity and 'the Light' helped raise that Courier to a higher percentage of frequency. So much of all this was on-the-job training. I welcomed it!"

At last, after this final rather esoteric panic, everything was ready. As the sun carved its way across the heavens on a promisingly beautiful day, we watched what would prove to be the most astonishing of all our ventures so far draw ever closer.

Ascent

We had all agreed to meet in the car park of the *Jack and Jill* pub at Clayton for 7.00pm. From there we would share cars, make our way up the track which ran alongside the appropriately-named *Three Greys* riding stables ('grey' being the adopted name for certain types of alleged ETs) and carry on up the hill toward Wolstonbury.

Looking back along the path to Wolstonbury from Clayton, the famous 'Jack and Jill' windmills visible in the distance - another entry in our long-distance disabled psychic-ferrying record attempt!

As our vehicles gathered conspicuously on the tarmac at the back of the pub, so the suspicions of the landlord were aroused. A figure strode into view and his body language wasn't friendly. Confronting us, he demanded to know what we were doing in his car park. "I'm sick of people using this as some kind of public lay-by while they go gallivanting off across the downs," he said, or words to that effect, adding pointedly; "Or are you here to have a *drink?*". Actually, we had every intention of gracing his pint glasses with our lips, but *after* we had come down from Wolstonbury. We decided to come clean and told him that were indeed off to 'gallivant' but that we would definitely return to patronise his pub. Eyeing us with a penetrating glare, he reluctantly let us go, uncertain whether or not to believe us.

Karen and Jason took Steve down to Saddlescombe to set up his video and arranged to meet us later at the top of Wolstonbury. The remainder of us crammed into two cars and made our bumpy way up the track as far as we could before having to get out on foot - or wheels in Paul's case. A gate barred the way further for vehicles. From here our site was about a quarter of a mile west but at least the path was dry and easy. The evening sun shone with a golden glow. We had been 'lucky' with the weather again although as we got higher up the slopes the wind rose and the temperature noticeably dropped - a bane for those of us dressed in shorts and T-shirts!

It wasn't possible to sit on the very summit of Wolstonbury, it was too bumpy for wheelchairs, but the spot we chose was close enough. From up here we had a magnificent view of the countryside vista below us, dissolving into glowing mist as the sun fell lower. Arriving at the area I had surveyed two weeks earlier, we needed to find the exact location of the energy line so we could sit in our chosen places on the Couriers. David and Michael set to work with their dowsing rods. Using pebbles, we marked out the position where each person should sit. Unfortunately, we weren't so lucky with privacy this year. The energy line crossed the main bridleway and we were placed just back from the path, facing towards Saddlescombe a mile or so away.

Setting up at the top of Wolstonbury, David dowses for the positions where we would sit on the energy lines, marked with rocks and pebbles. Photo: Barry Reynolds

Martin and David locating the 'Courier' lines. Photo: Barry Reynolds

As he dowsed, David noticed something very odd, the significance of which we would not recognise that evening. The direction of the Couriers' energy flows seemed to alternate. The first was flowing outwards to our designated site as planned but the next was coming back *towards* Wolstonbury. And so on throughout the lines. There seemed little we could do about it. We decided to press on regardless.

Iron, Fire And Water

Jason and Karen returned from their trip to Saddlescombe just before 8.20pm, Steve now ensconced for his lonely vigil with the video camera. We had about twenty five minutes before the sun would touch the curve of the horizon, which we could see perfectly from up here. It was time for Paul, Jason and I to conduct the ritual which the information from Elle had seemed to suggest. Not far from our marked positions were three indistinct tumuli, presumably burial mounds, set back from the path just within reach behind a wire fence. In Paul's mind this was what Elle had described as "*Many lie there. With marks, without marks. Between two...*" Leaving the others setting up we made our way to the mounds. By now, despite the clear skies, a strong wind was blowing steadily. Yet a stillness seemed to fall as Paul began our invocation and cerise light from the setting sun created a magical atmosphere:

"Whilst David and Michael pin-pointed the exact position of each Courier line, Andy, Jason and I stole quietly away. The wheelchair bumped and creaked its way toward the ancient tumuli. It was at these small hillocks of internment that we played

The tumuli at which Paul, Jason and Andy conducted the opening ritual at Wolstonbury, an action which was to have an instant effect on the Courier lines.

out our pre-meditation ritual. I could feel the presence of Damus every step of the way, his strength, his certainty, his encouragement. I needed it too. Again I was the unwitting focal point of this seemingly outrageous adventure."

"It was impossible to get the wheelchair beyond the wire that separated us from the mounds but we could get close enough to play out the task. It seemed imperative to the main event. To Jason I gave the iron stone, to Andy the holy water, and for myself the fire stone and a small written invocation to Lady Ellen (Joeb's beloved Ayesha). The three of us crowded near the edge of the mound nearest the fence. I read the invocation... and then there were four! Suddenly, and with great power, Damus, carrying his long staff, made his presence known to me. At a given point Jason buried his iron stone. In turn I buried the fire stone. I then directed Andy to sprinkle the holy water as a kind of catalyst, the final ingredient. I felt Damus raise his mighty staff, plunging it deep into the earth; at the same time my own arm raised up as a shadow of what he did and I felt the power and love of this simple act, felt the staff in my hand, its descent and meaning. It was a 'seal' breaking, and later I was to realise it was a promise also, as much as it was when Damus first struck the oak and swore to protect this beautiful place!"

"It was done. What we had achieved was a kind of alchemical blending of frequencies, resulting in a shattering of a seal placed on this site long ago, protecting ancient esoteric knowledge from dark hands. Now it was up and running, sharing what it knew with those who would listen. Elle had broken a few more of the bonds that held her. She was breaking free!"

"We made our way back to the main party. "I don't know what you did over there, Paul," said David, "but the Courier lines just shot up in number from nine to eighteen and then up to twenty-seven!" Something had been released... and was stirring from its slumber."

Don't be fooled by the sunshine - it was cold up on Wolstonbury, hence Linda is wrapped in plastic sheeting. Note how close our positions were to the barbed wire which bordered the main bridlepath. Photo: Barry Reynolds

Sundown

At 8.45pm we took our positions, the deep orange ball of the sun hovering just above the distant hills. A blanket of dusky red lay on the horizon as far as the eye could see, the fields and houses far below us now just shadows. With our only heat source about to vanish, it grew even colder. We would have to sit for twenty minutes. I lent Paul my sweater - I had brought other layers but Barry was left to freeze in his Bermudas.

Paul opened with a short invocation he had prepared a few days earlier and allowed Damus to come through again:

"The invocation that I had worked on days before was to Lord Michael (archangel Michael, or at least that stream of consciousness to which the name had been given). As we were working so closely with the Devic forces it seemed fitting that we address this great being."

"We called on him, Lord of the Angels of Light and mediator between the human race and the Devic forces. We made our request for their co-operation with our project and that it be granted. I asked that Damus would be supported in his work, that we be guided and sustained, that all this be done in the name of the Light."

"We were now in the hands of something mystical and profound, beyond mind and body. Where were we going and would we ever arrive?"

At 8.47pm, the sun finally appeared to touch the Earth, sinking into gathering purple gloom. At this, using a portable ghetto-blaster, we switched on the tape of the musical notes which Paul had divined and Martin had prepared. The odd high-pitched warble filled the air all around us, reverberating inside our heads not unpleasantly but hypnotically. With that and the invocation, we had indeed brought "*Song* (of sorts) *and word*".

Holding the crystals we had each been designated, we visualised opening our minds as if a flower were unfolding above our heads. We imagined a bright golden light flowing down into our crowns, through our bodies. Allowing this light to stream from the solar plexus into the crystal in our hands, from here each of us focused it into our own Courier line, feeling the light coursing through the Earth itself, towards our wheat field and into the etheric pattern held there.

Four frames from the video sequence of the Wolstonbury experiment: Paul, holding his crystal, channels 'Damus' as the sun descends behind him, ready to start the meditation as it touches the horizon.

What a sight we must have been; nine people lined up next to a public footpath, eyes closed, crystals in hand, away with the fairies (perhaps literally?) while a tape recorder pumped out a bizarre whistling sound. Unlike Cissbury the year before, where all had stayed away, a number of hikers and horse riders passed by, laughing and shaking their heads.

But what did we care? The meditation was a beautiful and fulfilling experience. There was a real sense of power flowing through us. We had become simple but vital conductors for something far greater, valves in a huge mechanism the nature of which we could never truly comprehend. Even the by now biting cold was forgotten while we drifted, our minds in free-fall.

At 9.10pm, almost in unspoken agreement, we began to emerge from our contemplation, turning to each other. Damus came through and with a few words of blessing, what would turn out to be our last - and most significant - experience as a group together was over.

With the sun gone, the light was fading fast and it was time to pack up and make our way down before darkness fell. David did a quick re-dowse of the energy line. To his amazement, it had now expanded even further and had split into seventy-two parts! Whatever we had achieved by being there, it had not gone unnoticed by the local energy grid. Something was happening.

Descent

Full of nervous expectations, we made our way back to the cars, freezing but somehow satisfied that we had played a part in some wider scheme, whether or not we got a crop formation out of it. We wondered how Steve had fared. Had he witnessed anything? In stark contrast to the red sunburn of the previous year, Karen was almost blue with cold by the time we got under cover of the vehicles. We were all glad of the shelter.

Jason and Karen set off to retrieve Steve, to join us later. The rest of us returned to the *Jack and Jill* and kept our promise to patronise the landlord's premises! In fact, by the time we got there we were gasping for liquid refreshment. Well, some of us. Michael and David scuttled off and Paul, exhausted clairvoyantly and physically, made his own excuses and left for home. We could see the look of surprise in the landlord's eyes and sensed that we had restored a little of his faith in humanity by returning as promised. After his earlier hostility, he treated us like old friends.

Steve and his search party finally turned up. He hadn't seen or heard anything unusual as he waited by the field at Saddlescombe but we didn't feel too disappointed. If something were to happen there any time from now, this year, the next or whenever, we would have every right to suspect that our work on Wolstonbury had something to do with it. Now all we could do was wait.

Later that night, when the pub had closed and all was dark and still, Jason and I returned to hold a little private sitting at our field. It seemed the thing to do, a mark of respect almost. The stars glowed brightly above. We sat on the grassy bank overlooking the whispering wheat and talked quietly, discussing our hopes and fears for the project and realising somehow that a watershed had been reached, that our work of the previous three years was essentially over. Yet we still awaited a... *result*.

Despite our earnest wishes, nothing wonderful happened in the field below us as we spoke, but we were happy, if not quite contented. It was time to leave. As we walked to the cars, parked under trees in pitch shadow, we became aware of little points of light glowing like green jewels in the long grass. We were witnessing a rare sight in these times of extinction - glow worms. Somehow, their bright bodies lifted our spirits and we left for home, full of hope.

We were still waiting for our 'result' - we wouldn't have to wait long. Even as we stood in the jewelled darkness, it was manifesting itself. But things weren't happening quite as expected and we would not be returning to Saddlescombe...

Walking the circles and rings which appeared at Felbridge on the night of the Wolstonbury experiment. Photo: Barry Reynolds

10: SIX CIRCULAR ELEMENTS

The veins of energy which spread like branches across the land were pulsing with a new input of light, this time from a source which felt less familiar. Yet the psychic needle which injected the light had pressed against part of the flow. There was a resistance to the pulse reaching its intended destination. The lines knew better and flowed the fuse potential to another, more comfortable junction.

Isolated and dark, a field awoke, sensing the inrush. Suddenly a circuit was complete. The etheric blueprint which contained myriad possibilities of shape and form was filled with light, defining its configuration. Realities inverted, met and interfaced. Thousands of living stems fell on command and rings and circles lived.

Night Shift

Coming down from his psychic efforts at the Wolstonbury experiment the night before, Paul spent an uncomfortable day waiting for the telephone to ring. Although he was prepared for things to take a while to happen, he was still afraid that all our work might come to nothing. The phone remained stubbornly silent. Yet on going to bed his slumber was disturbed and he was visited by messages and visions:

"I began to think I was caught up in another psychic dead-end. But maybe not. That night I couldn't sleep. There was no reason for that until I realised someone wanted to speak with me. I turned on my back and 'opened up'. It was Damus. He said: "*You have done far more than you know. The number nine Courier line has now risen from twenty-five per cent up to forty per cent.*" I suddenly became aware that Lady Ellen was also present. She told me about three crop circles that had been formed. She was smiling warmly. I was tired and wanted to sleep but this information was so strong."

"The next morning I awoke refreshed and immediately dowsed the ninth Courier line. It had risen in effectiveness just as Damus had said. I couldn't believe it! I tried to phone David to check. He was out. I left a message on Jason's answering machine to do a dowse and call me back. I phoned my fellow dowser Hilda Bell and asked her to check it out also - without leading her. Hilda was the first to come back. She confirmed my findings; the energy had risen to at least forty per cent! Jason also got back to me and again there was a confirmation. But I needed to hear it from David. He called at last and decided to dowse there and then over the phone. David got forty per cent! I asked him to check whether this was global. I heard him mutter "You bugger!" He told me that the pendulum swung backwards and forwards, which meant neither yes or no. Later Jason tried it and got the same result but when asked whether the energy was spreading around the Earth's grid he got a 'yes'."

It seemed that not only had we split the Wolstonbury energy line into many extra parts (although presumably not working to capacity yet) but our placing of Karen on the ninth Courier had substantially raised its activity even if we couldn't be sure how far-reaching the effect was.

A Voice From The Past

On Friday 30th June, Barry received a telephone call from a farmer we had previously had dealings with in 1993. Back then, one of his fields at Felbridge, near East Grinstead in West Sussex, had been visited by an elaborate pictogram of rings and pathways. He was kind enough to let some of the CCCS Sussex team in to survey it just before he harvested. Although agnostic over the origins of the design, he had rather enjoyed the attention it brought and appeared proudly standing in the formation on the front page of the local newspaper.

Now crop circles had returned to the same field. For the first time ever, we had an excited farmer contacting *us* with the news! 1995 had already been a busy year for the phenomenon in Sussex. There had been three crop designs since May and this simply sounded like the latest instalment. We had hoped that the next might be discovered at Saddlescombe but this clearly wasn't to be. When the farmer described the new pattern and the date it appeared, however, Barry's suspicions were immediately aroused...

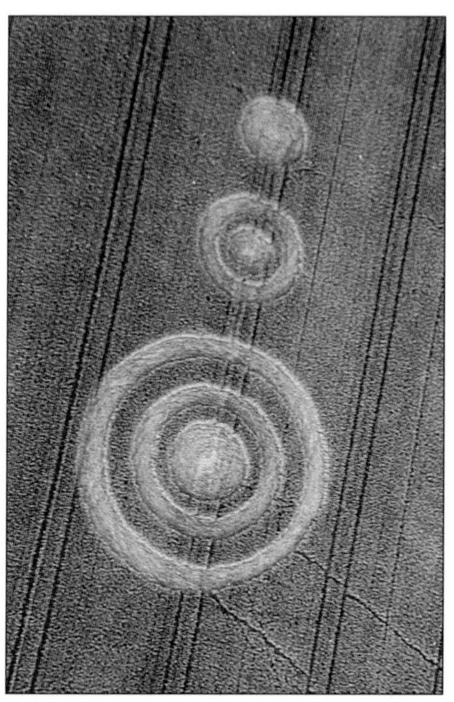

The Felbridge rings as seen from the air... The very pattern Barry had predicted might result from our meditation.

The Wolstonbury Legacy

The telephone lines between the members of the team were suddenly red hot. The Felbridge formation had appeared the very night we were out meditating on the 28th June. It was discovered by one of the farm workers on the morning of the 29th. The field had been passed by staff several times the day before and nothing was there. This date of arrival was in itself uncanny but it was the following piece of information which raised shivers up the spine of each of us in turn as the news was relayed...

The design consisted of SIX CIRCULAR ELEMENTS of different sizes, a small single circle above a larger circle with one standing ring, above a still larger circle with two standing rings. These were the features which Barry had suggested might result from the playing of the musical notes at the Wolstonbury experiment. There was no ambiguity here - they had appeared in EXACTLY the pattern Barry had sketched at the meeting with Damus, of which we had thought so little at the time. There was no doubt about it - this was *our* formation.

With rising excitement, Paul now began to understand the message from Lady Ellen:

"I kept wondering about Lady Ellen and the *three* circles. I mean, I was delighted with the finding of the one formation but where were the other two she had spoken of? Perhaps they just hadn't been discovered - or perhaps they hadn't been created yet! Barry phoned to tell me more of the new pattern. His prediction and drawing of "six circular elements" did indeed correspond with the six rings and circles found in the formation, each being of a different size and resonance! I asked Barry to tell me, as I hadn't had a chance to visit it yet, *exactly* what the formation looked like. He described *three separate circles* riding due east-west. "Did you say three *separate* circles?" I said, "I mean not superimposed on one another?" "That's right," he replied, "one circle at the top, the second underneath containing a single ring within it and a third circle containing two rings." "So that's what she meant!" I almost shouted. "She meant three crop circles IN THE SAME FIELD!" I wasn't going barmy after all. But to cap it all, and for my money this put the lid on it, we had three circles that seemingly corresponded to the six musical notes, the very sound that we had played during that wild and windy time atop Wolstonbury Hill. My joy knew no bounds. I whooped and screamed. Now was a time to let off some of the steam that had built within me. Suddenly it had all come together. This was it. WE HAD DONE IT!"

There was just one problem. What the hell was our formation doing up at *Felbridge* several miles away and not Saddlescombe?

A Conundrum

On realising the significance of the Felbridge rings, Barry immediately reached for his Ordnance Survey maps. Taking a ruler, he placed one end at Saddlescombe, took it through the heart of Wolstonbury Hill where we had sat and then extended it further to see where it would go. A direct line ran from our two sites and on right through to... Felbridge.

Now we remembered David's observation while dowsing our positions up on Wolstonbury, about the alternating directions of the energy flows in the Courier lines. The light we had channelled had gone not southward to Saddlescombe but backwards up to Felbridge. On hearing the news of our success, David reached for his own maps and dowsing implements. To his astonishment, not only were the three sites of Saddlescombe, Wolstonbury and Felbridge geographically aligned, as Barry had discovered, but they were also connected by an already existing *energy* line that fed directly into the field with the formation. We had only concentrated on the section which connected our two sites. We hadn't considered that it might extend northward from the other side of Wolstonbury. By ignoring the alternating flows of the Couriers at the time of our meditation, we had tried to force our thought-pulses in a direction they clearly didn't want to go that night.

But why had the energy gone the opposite way? One thing which none of us had considered when Paul first began to seek an etheric blueprint was whether or not that particular junction was *ready* to be triggered. Maybe ours had been too old or needed greater preparation before the likes of us could fire it up. After all, there had been no crop formations in that area for several years. Given this, perhaps the energy we were focusing into the line had simply reached out for the nearest location that *was* available for active work, like lightning seeking the fastest way to earth itself. The field at Felbridge had been host to a pictogram only two years previously, just yards away from the new design, and may have been the first attractive stopping point for our light injection. And for all we knew, the Guardians and Devas may have played their part in re-routing our misdirected efforts to somewhere more useful.

That Barry had visualised the crop pattern on the basic inspiration of the six musical notes and that this very shape had appeared but not where we thought it would seemed to confirm that the junction points weren't set in their configurations. Each one could be manipulated to produce many shapes. Circles often recurred on exactly the same sites as previous years' events but in different configurations, suggesting that there were energy collection points which could hold many, maybe unlimited, patterns and that these could be determined by the influx of energy from a variety of sources, be they natural (perhaps in the case of simple circles), extra-terrestrial, Devic or human. Our concentration, the crystals and the sine wave chord, in this instance, had somehow combined to create a design of six circular elements on a spot of infinite possibilities.

Dawning Realisation

It took a while for the enormity of what we had apparently achieved to sink in; indeed we couldn't really believe there was an 'apparently' to it. Apart from all the obvious signs, we each instinctively *knew* we had played a part in the creation of this event. We couldn't be sure how much of the formation's appearance was due to us and how much to behind the scenes work from other forces but we felt certain that without our input the Felbridge pictogram would not be there in that configuration. As the field had been visited before, cynics could write off its arrival as coincidence, but as we had learned, coincidence was a word which no longer had any meaning for something as obviously interactive as the crop circles and their associated phenomena.

Despite all the remarkable things which had happened to us during the course of our four years' work, we had still lacked the crowning glory of something tangible to show for it. But now, at last, we had the 'result' we craved.

Yet we realised sceptics would never accept a word of this. Indeed, it was highly likely it would be suggested that the formation at Felbridge was hoaxed either by ourselves or others. We all trusted each other enough to know that none of the team would ever try to dupe the others by trudging out the rings one night and the outside world would have to trust us that we hadn't conspired together to give our project a credible climax (we hadn't). If it were to turn out that *someone else* outside of the group had created the pictogram, it would simply add even more strangeness and synchronicity to the whole experiment. That they would have created *that* design on *that* night on *that* part of the energy line would have to suggest they were being guided by mysterious forces far beyond a mischievous human intent and we would still have our 'result' regardless. No-one outside of the group knew a thing about where and when we were carrying out our work, nor what we expected from it. In any case, the rings displayed no trace of blatant human activity.

The warnings of Jeuz still rang in our heads though and we were realistic about the chances of ever convincing the world that, for one evening at least, we ourselves had interacted with - or become - the circle-makers. We may not have videoed the crucial moment but by now had learnt our lesson about 'proving' things and our aspirations had moved on from the simplistic aims we had started with. We had learned many things over the years, about ourselves, how to work together effectively as a team, how to accept failure, and about the hidden capabilities of human beings, physically, spiritually and psychically - and we had only scratched the surface. Most of all, we had learnt that the Universe was a far stranger place than most of us had ever imagined and in some directions were left with more questions than answers. Proving all this to anyone would be impossible. But it didn't matter. We had persevered and been rewarded. *We* knew what we had achieved.

Linda and family explore the Felbridge formation. These photos show how crisply defined the pattern was. Photo: Barry Reynolds

Walking The 'Result'

To finally stand inside what was effectively the end product of four summers' joy, passion and heartache was a humbling and moving experience. The formation was beautiful, less complex than many of the intricate and profound symbols which were falling from nowhere onto the fields of the world, yet somehow satisfying in its simplicity. The rings were extremely clear-cut and the lay of the still green long-eared wheat was neat and attractive. Such was the finesse of the artistry involved, at the edge of the largest circle we found individual stems which had been pulled into the flow of the laid crop from *behind* unaffected standing plants.

We couldn't have asked for more ideal circumstances or a better location for the pattern, perhaps another reason why our intents were guided elsewhere and not to Saddlescombe. Here we had a farmer who was friendly and enthusiastic enough to let us know about the formation's arrival and welcomed our presence, a situation which might not have arisen at our chosen site, where the landowner's demeanour was uncertain.

The huge field which held the design was a gorgeous spot, bordered by trees on three sides and conveniently isolated, with no roads in the vicinity and only the Worth Way footpath which passed through nearby woods from which it could be glimpsed. No-one would disturb our personal contemplations or surveying activities as we walked the maze of rings. Only aeroplanes from nearby Gatwick broke the peace as they ascended on their journeys above and even they seemed distant enough not to matter.

Around the edge of the standing wheat, a strip of grass bordered all sides of the field. This gave the fortunate side effect of making it possible to drive right up to the area with the pictogram, saving a long walk through narrow tractor lines. Long walks were something out of the question for Paul - so here he was being given an opportunity to inspect for himself the fruits of what had begun at his house that wind-swept night in 1992.

One warm July evening, with the sun low in the sky casting gold light and long shadows, Jason and I drove with Paul to Felbridge. Enjoying the novelty of the bumpy ride into the field, we pulled up near the formation. Paul could be carried the fifty feet or so across the standing crop. Some of us had already visited the site many times but for Paul he was inside an actual crop formation for only the second time in his life - and this time he understood something of its origins:

"It wasn't just that these were the three circles that Lady Ellen promised, or the fact that they corresponded with Barry's prediction. No, it was more than that. Much more personal. Getting into a crop formation for me was almost impossible. They were usually in absolutely inaccessible places for a 'raspberry ripple' like me. But not this formation. Here, a person such as myself could drive right up to the edge of the circles. This had never happened before."

"Jason piggy-backed me into the formation, the wheelchair followed and I plonked myself down in it. Andy, Jason and I had grown very close over the years and I looked upon them as brothers. We sat with the silence, playing with it, listening to the roar of its welcome. We were at the other end of three long years of frustration and yearning, sitting in something very beautiful, something magical, a magic that had been lost these many centuries. I silently welcomed it back where it belonged and gave thanks to all those involved."

With the Felbridge event, at last we had something tangible to show for all our efforts. By now it didn't matter if no-one believed that we had played a metaphysical part in its creation - WE were content.

Before we left, never to return to our formation again, it seemed wrong not to do one final thing - have a chat with the local Guardian. We settled in the middle of the single-ringed circle and let our minds drift into relaxation as the sun sank below the trees. A peace fell. Soon a kindly, gentle voice spoke through Paul. We couldn't resist a smile when he announced himself as 'Kirk'. Paul told us later that he visualised him as a tall Scotsman, not captain of the starship *Enterprise*. However...

"I thought of Captain Kirk and all that implied. We laughed at the concept. I remember thinking that it was laughter that had seen us through. What would we have done without humour? I for one would have gone mad. One thing I learned from the entities that I had been privileged to be a channel for was that they all, once you got to know them, had a wonderful sense of humour. The Cosmos must ring with the laughter of countless beings. I wonder whether there is a common cosmic joke that we can all share, one that rings out amongst the stars. I wonder."

Kirk spoke of the beauty of the place he was assigned to and of his feelings of pride that the circles had chosen to visit his home once more. In keeping with the distance of the other Guardians we had talked to, Kirk knew little about what had created the pattern, only that, in this case, the impetus which made it had not come from this area. We explained our role in its creation and the effect on the local energy grid and he was pleased, almost proud of us.

With the sun gone and the shadows closing in, we knew it was time to leave, somehow realising, as we turned our back on that field for the last time, that our primary work together was over and an era had passed.

Closing Signs

As if to confirm that we had finally reached the level of interaction we had sought for so long, we received one more gift from the circle-making forces in 1995. On 15th July, a huge multi-ringed crop formation appeared at the foot of Cissbury Ring, its off-centre geometry resembling a hypnotic tunnel into the Earth. Ten days later a circle, triangle and an elaborate dumbbell appeared next to it.

Despite being the power source for all the Sompting patterns and the centre of our work with the Guardians and Jeuz in 1994, never before had a crop glyph arrived so close to the ancient hill itself. Maybe its manifestation was just that strained concept 'coincidence' but we took it as a sign of acknowledgement to our efforts, a final nod of thanks. It was certainly one of the most ambitious and beautiful crop designs Sussex had ever seen.

The huge formation which appeared at the foot of Cissbury Ring (top of picture) in July 1995 - a final nod of acknowledgement from the circle-making forces?

And at the site of our most recent experiment, it seemed a legacy had been left behind. Wolstonbury Hill had been the site of sporadic UFO reports

The Cissbury formation from the air ... an exquisite gift. Photo: Michael Hubbard

Rings at the Ring. As ever with crop patterns, the scale of the Cissbury formation could only be really appreciated from within. Photo: Steve Alexander

before but from the summer of 1995 onwards it became a local hotspot for sightings of strange glowing lights in the sky. Many claimed to have witnessed these hovering over and around its summit. Given that throughout our communication exercises light phenomena had apparently been generated around certain key members of the group, perhaps our work at Wolstonbury had not only given birth to a crop formation but had also unlocked radiant energies through our expansion of the local Courier grid - or encouraged visitors from the skies.

One last, amusing, synchronous event was to occur. I found myself speaking about the Wolstonbury experiment on *BBC Southern Counties Radio* a few months later. In the studio the next guest on the show was waiting to talk on an entirely different subject. As I went to leave, he caught my arm - and informed me that he was the livestock owner who farmed the downs of Wolstonbury Hill... Luckily he was intrigued, not upset, by the work we carried out there!

The Curtain Falls

We had each suspected deep down that the Wolstonbury experiment might be the last time we would all work together as a team for 'communication' purposes. If nothing had resulted from it we would probably have given up the concept of interaction with the circle-making forces as a good idea which we didn't have the skill or understanding to pull off properly. Yet now there had been a firm resolution to our work, where could we go from here?

When the significance of the Felbridge formation and the other effects of our meditation finally sank in and we became aware that we had achieved all we could reasonably hope for, there was little impetus left to continue the project. We could keep going, perhaps triggering other energy junction points, but what would that prove, beyond that which we had already proved to ourselves? We were satisfied that the human mind played a role in the process of whatever ultimately created the crop circles. We had indeed interacted and communicated with the phenomenon and fulfilled our quest for contact.

We could persevere in the hope that we might finally get the video of a formation appearing that we had originally set out for but Jeuz or whatever energy had spoken through Paul had shown us the folly of trying to force things on a disbelieving world. On a personal level it would be monumentally exciting to witness such a sight but in many ways we already had enough to satisfy us of the phenomenon's unphysical nature. Was it worth more, possibly long, years of struggle, however enlightening, only to be ridiculed and debunked if we were eventually successful? Given the way they usually seemed to work, the circle-making forces, as our communications had defined them, would grant us a glimpse of their craftsmanship in action if deemed necessary. If not, it was clearly something we could live without.

It wasn't that we were disillusioned in any way. On the contrary, we were happy and contented with what we had achieved and it felt right to leave things at that. If we got the urge to carry out further experiments then we would. If not, we would sleep sound in the knowledge that we had once attempted something ambitious and extraordinary from which we had learnt.

Other information had been forthcoming which would perhaps prove of use in the future - or become redundant. What of Joeb's predictions of Earth changes? Would his original visions of disastrous upheaval, however positive the eventual outcome, come to pass? Or had our and many, many people's efforts in working positively with the planet, spiritually and environmentally, averted this scenario as Joeb had said might be possible? Only time would tell.

For now, it seemed we had attained all we could on this level. Paul, the hub and inspiration for so much of our communication work, felt as instinctively as everyone else that our work in this direction was done:

"And so the curtain fell on four years of drama and fears, joy and hidden tears. A time of vast change, a time of pursuit, a time of challenge, a time of wonder. A change occurred in all of us concerned with this quest, sometimes subtle, sometimes profound. It was also a time of glory, frustration and sometimes downright blindness! It had been a challenge to continually try harder, find another tack, look in another direction, take notice of dreams and intuition, never to let go of the pursuit of truth."

"Even if I had found that all I held dear was a lie, complete junk, a blind alley, then I would have said "Okay, I was wrong. But I'll keep on looking, keep on keeping on until I find the chunk of the jigsaw that's missing, the piece that will bring together this vast, beautiful and sometimes painful journey called life". I believe that the truth itself never changes, only our perception of it."

"But in all that we learned, or think we learned, I believe that we took a closer look at OURSELVES. The circles and the circle-makers played their part in that. In all our chasing and probing we were also probing inwardly, pulling out parts of our spiritual selves that perhaps would have remained hidden. This, after all, in my opinion, and indeed that of Joeb, is what the circles are for: to open up the minds of humankind to a greater reality of what is and what is to come."

"For my part this had been a spiritual quest and in their heart-of-hearts I believe that all my fellow questers would say the same. My life had now changed forever. Thank God!"

"But where would we have been without the help, wisdom and guidance of certain unseen forces, which once again in the vast history of this planet are making themselves known? These intelligences become as familiar to you as radio waves when you begin to expand your awareness of mind and spirit and realise they exist."

"I pay tribute to Andy for being my good friend, his continued faith in my abilities (well, most of the time) and for never losing site of our goal. I salute him. I also give grateful thanks to my good and faithful friend Joeb. To Emun, Tryst and Rachael of Cissbury Ring. To Armis and Cened. To Jeuz of the star system Sirius. To Damus of the Whistling Hill. Lastly, I thank Ayesha, the spirit of the Earth. May they prosper and grow. May we ALL prosper and grow in the light of love."

The End..?

By the summer of 1996, Paul had plans to follow his family up to Anglesey. He had closed his health food business and his departure, whenever it came, would mark the end of an adventure that began with a curiosity about the symbols which were appearing in the fields of our home county and beyond. Once the house of the saucers was sold, the weekly meetings with Joeb would come to an end and those who had gathered for advice and information would be scattered to spread their acquired knowledge to others. With the uncertainty about Paul's move in the air, there was no way any further experiments could be planned even if anyone had wanted to and we were content to let it lie until such time the spark came again.

Curiously, despite the survey team being ever-alert, the crop formations Sussex received in 1996, though attractive in their way, were fewer than in recent summers and seemed muted in their design. Most of the eleven which did appear seemed to do so within a two-week period from the end of July. The return to far simpler patterns after such a breathtaking array in 1995 made some of us wonder, perhaps a little arrogantly, if this was the phenomenon responding in kind to the lack of interactive activity on our part. Or was it that an end had been achieved in this area which meant that elaborate crop formations were no longer necessary for the time being?

When our adventures began, most of us had no idea what we were letting ourselves in for, nor exactly how psychic communication would work in connection with the phenomenon we were researching. We had taken the word of Joeb and the Guardians on trust, to see where this particular 'path of possibilities' would take us. By the end, those who took part in the process had formed their own ideas as to the true nature of the communicants and the integrity of the information we had been given, or they remained open-minded. But all agreed that the path *had* lead somewhere worthwhile and our lives had been enriched as a result. Our work in this direction was over for the moment. Now it was time to take our experiences and learning and share them with the outside world. The writing of this book is part of that sharing.

But 1996 had one more lesson for us, in an event which would throw into sharp relief one of the major insights we had received from our four-year quest...

Whitewashed and boarded up. With the closure of Paul's business, it was only a matter of time before he followed his family to Anglesey. A very special era of our lives was over, but we were happy.

The Oliver's Castle formation 1996 from the side of the ancient hill-fort, a view very similar to that seen in the video which purports to show this pattern appearing under arcing lights...

EPILOGUE:
OLIVER'S TWIST

In the early hours of Sunday August 11th 1996, a large and elaborate crop formation appeared in a wheat field at the foot of the Iron Age hill-fort Oliver's Castle, near Devizes in Wiltshire. Nearly three hundred feet across, six thin arms extended from a large central circle, each culminating in a dumbbell with a small circle perched at the tip. The design resembled, and was instantly dubbed, a 'snowflake'.

Like Cissbury Ring, Oliver's Castle is a huge embankment sculpted from an outcrop of downland and from it a glorious vista unfolds of the fields below. From this vantage point, in the early hours of dawn on the day of the formation's appearance, a young man in his early twenties claimed he was out looking for crop circles and UFOs, which in years past had occurred or been reported at this spot before (the CSETI meditation-inspired symbol appeared near here).

According to *his* testimony, as the sky lightened on a morning of drizzle, his attention was drawn to one of the fields below by a noise like high-pitched "crickets". In it was a strange light. He reached for his camcorder. As he filmed, the snowflake crop pattern unfolded in front of him beneath a series of glowing white lights arcing across the wheat.

Later that day, the young man took his video to the popular drinking haven of crop circle researchers, *The Barge* at Honeystreet, near Alton Barnes. A group of people viewed his astonishing footage. It appeared to show two rapidly flying incandescent globes turning a tight circle over the field in view. As they passed across the centre, maybe thirty feet or so above the crop, the snowflake began to appear below, different parts of its design materialising as if out of nowhere and then linking up to complete the whole. Another glowing light then came into view and split into two as it passed over the middle of the developing pattern. These, like the first pair, then arced around and moved swiftly out of sight, one accelerating away from the other. The entire sequence was approximately eighteen seconds long. The formation was seen to appear within seven seconds.

To the amazement of all who saw the footage, this person had apparently managed to video what no-one had ever yet achieved - on-camera evidence of a crop formation being created by non-human forces. Nobody knew what the glowing lights were or why they behaved as they did but they were consistent with phenomena which had been seen and videoed on other occasions, including that seen by members of our team. Here at last appeared to be the proof. Now the world would have to sit up and take notice of this incredible phenomenon. Wouldn't it?

As copies of the video were distributed around the crop circle research 'community', initial excitement quickly began to give way to scepticism. Suddenly, for some, it all seemed too good to be true. A curious logic set in; they thought it showed too much of what researchers would *expect* to see - therefore it was fake, a computer simulation. The picture was too clear, the formation too conveniently near centre-frame. Why didn't the cameraman follow the lights as they flew off? There were some valid questions to be asked about the footage but abruptly many people's objectivity took a tumble into oblivion. Their cynicism began to rub off onto others. Second-hand opinions and fourth-hand information were now bandied about as absolutes. There was no proof but it didn't matter, the video WAS fake. No question about it. Couldn't possibly be real. How could anyone ever have been fooled in the first place? Those initially impressed, who had splashed the story the loudest, claimed they were never really taken in. They had suspected the 'truth' all along. Talk of dark conspiracies arose. Some asserted the intelligence services were involved. It was all part of some plan or vendetta to catch out and discredit certain individuals. Private detectives were hired. Complex webs of tangled circumstances were supposed and presented as fact. Home computer enthusiasts knocked up their own versions of formations being created to show how easy such a sequence would be to create. They looked nothing like the original footage, but what matter? Yes, to its detractors, who spread their gospel far and wide, there was no doubt about it, the Oliver's Castle video, though impressive to the eye, was a fabrication, plain and simple.

There were those who disagreed and pointed to unexplained aspects of the video - many expert technical analysts were unable to find anything which betrayed it as having been tampered with in any way. How could the sequence have been created so quickly given that it was first shown on the same day the formation appeared? There were subtleties to the way the balls of light behaved which seemed too meticulous for a hastily-created fake. Where was the final, unequivocal *proof* that the footage was deceitfully invented?

But those who dared to raise such enquiries in support of the video's possible authenticity were instantly ridiculed, even by some normally sober researchers, and condemned as fundamentalist fanatics uninterested in the truth, only articles of faith. Those who tried to put a balanced view and remain open-minded were dragged down by the anti-brigade and paraded as naive advocates. The accepted wisdom was by now that the video was a hoax - as indeed, by implication, was the formation, now described by some as a total mess despite the fact it was as impressive as several other major patterns from 1996 which had been accepted as 'genuine', and displayed many of the same

"You can turn the whole world upside down and they will not believe you..." Standing in the Oliver's Castle 'snowflake', dismissed as a shambolic mess by those eager to debunk the video and the formation, most of whom never visited it. You decide.

qualities. The unfortunate, and admittedly odd, unavailability of the cameraman for questioning was seen as the final nail in the snowflake video's by now well-built coffin.

Total polarisation had been reached. And all this before the story even reached the mass-media. Those in the anti-camp would now never accept any evidence that they might be wrong. Those who believed the video genuine would now never be convinced that any evidence *against* it being authentic was reliable given the hysterical scramble for conspiracy theories. As a result, the truth will probably never be agreed on.

The Oliver's Castle video has already passed into contentious legend and taken its place in the already confused pantheon of crop circle history. Whether it is truly fake or otherwise is impossible to say at the time of writing and is irrelevant to this book. It is the *reaction* to the arrival of such a sequence which is the concern of this epilogue.

It is now clear, in the wake of this event, how we as the Sussex communication team might have been treated had we achieved our original goal and been successful in producing a video of a formation manifesting out of thin air. The warning of Jeuz seems more pertinent than ever. What if, on the first rendezvous night on the slopes of Saddlescombe, that ring of blue lights glimpsed by three of our group had suddenly brightened and not faded away? What if, as we watched these glowing lights arcing over the barley, stems had really begun to fall and circles were created? What would have happened to us as a team and as individuals? With several camcorders activated we would have had the advantage of having more than one videotape to verify our experience but what would really have come of us and our great proof to the world of the phenomenon's viability?

The backlash against the Oliver's Castle video, which was condemned long before all or any of the facts were known gives us a pretty good clue as to what could have befallen. Chances are, we would have been pilloried as liars by those for whom anything which appears to circumvent the known laws of physics *can't* possibly exist, slated as frauds or deviants by envious members of the research 'community', ignored by most of the world which can't cope with thinking about things like that anyway and believed only by a few. It would have been discovered that at least two close contacts with our team worked in the video industry. We would have been accused of having faked our sequences using their equipment. Maybe the world would have been changed for a minority, but overall, life would have continued as before and we would be seen as nothing more than a group of eccentrics willing to fabricate anything to back up our belief-systems. Being younger, less savvy and perhaps a little more idealist than we are now, how many of us would have crumbled under the weight of such an onslaught? Perhaps, after all, we were not ready for that experience.

The Oliver's Castle fiasco has exposed gaping paradoxical cracks in the hopes and desires of many intrigued by the crop circle phenomenon. Presented with something that, if real, would be a major step forward in helping to draw attention to the potential importance of such an unexplained mystery, many turned their faces away without even *considering* that this new evidence might be what it seemed, whatever the truth. Sensible caution gave way to irrational debunking. If it turns out that the video is indeed a fabrication, these people will, on the surface, be vindicated - but at what cost to the integrity of our discernment processes? What are we going to do if a real sequence of such an event does actually come along? How will we recognise it if we insist on refusing to look closely at the evidence presented before reaching our conclusions, and open-mindedness is scorned?

Yet Steve Alexander had never been accused of faking his famous video of the ball of light at Alton Barnes. Of course, unlike the Oliver's Castle scenario, he was open and frank about his experience, as we would have been if we had obtained *our* video. But balls of light are one thing, crop circles visibly forming from nowhere are another. Perhaps that shatters too many perceptions, creates too much fear of the unknown. However open we might have been, would we have been spared the heavy guns?

Despite all the endless research and accumulated data which strongly suggests that the crop formations are something far beyond a human joke, there seems to be an inner reluctance to finally discover the true evidence of that. The crop circle research 'community' too often falls prey to self-destructive scepticism within its own ranks, based not on evidence but on fear of public ridicule - and something deeper. All the time the circles are beautiful, elusive patterns, simply out there to be romped in and photographed on a warm summer's day, there's a kind of safety in not knowing more. The thought that video or other final proof might arrive to conclusively show they are coming from a place resolutely *somewhere else* is perhaps too much for some. The reality of their true nature would be brought too close to the surface and the questions about their implications would suddenly become too uncomfortable.

Yet such a film may be produced tomorrow, assuming the existing one isn't it. Will footage taken in any circumstances, aside from that accompanying a simultaneous mass-witnessing, ever be treated more fairly than the controversial snowflake video? Will lessons be learned from the events of 1996 so that the next such evidence to come along will get a fairer hearing despite any concerns over its authenticity?

Whatever the conscious energy that called itself Jeuz was, it gave us a valuable piece of advice on that hot day at Cissbury which has relevance to all who would hope to reveal truths to the world that it would rather not have revealed. But with the warning came hope for those who believe in a deeper significance of the crop glyphs to a universal plan - that they are carrying out their task regardless of what is said or done against their name, immune to humankind's opinion of them:

"DO NOT PLACE SUCH IMPORTANCE ON THE PROOF! You are expanding. All those who are associated with these circles are expanding now and this is only the beginning. You will have proof with the corn but who will really believe you? You can turn the world upside down and they will not believe you.

Continue with your work, but do not be bogged down by trying to prove this or that because in the end IT MAKES NO DIFFERENCE - none!"

APPENDIX 1
USEFUL CONTACTS

SC - THE MONTHLY JOURNAL OF CROP CIRCLES AND BEYOND

Andy Thomas is editor of this publication, which has the largest annualised readership figures of any crop circle journal in the world. **SC** is one of the most influential sources of circle information. A monthly A5 booklet, it has readers across the globe and covers national and international events, as well as having extensive coverage of crop formations which appear in Sussex. Each issue contains up-to-the-minute news, reviews, reports and features on all the significant happenings in the circles world.

Subscription to **SC** is currently **£12.00** per year (UK), **£16.00** (Europe) and **£22.00** (non-US overseas). Currency for cheques and POs sent from abroad must be made out in Sterling, drawn on a bank with a British branch. If you would like to subscribe to **SC**, please send a cheque, payable to **SCR**, to the following address:

SC, 36 Graham Crescent, Mile Oak, Portslade, East Sussex, BN41 2YB, England. Tel: 01273 885117

USA subscriptions cost **$33.00** and cheques should be made payable to **'M Glickman'** please. Write to:

SC, PO Box 2077, Santa Monica, CA 90406-2077, USA.

SOUTHERN CIRCULAR RESEARCH/CCCS SUSSEX

Southern Circular Research, originally the Centre For Crop Circle Studies, Sussex branch, has been operating since 1991 and is one of the most active circle-investigation organisations in the world, gathering data from around the globe but in particular researching the appearance of crop formations in East and West Sussex. Still affiliated to CCCS, Southern Circular Research holds open meetings once a month, usually on the third Tuesday or Thursday of the month, at the following venue:

The Scout Centre, Station Road, Burgess Hill, West Sussex

The entrance to the Scout Centre can be found just opposite the *Potters Arms* public house. Meetings are held in the upper room, begin at 8.00pm and are usually a lively mixture of the latest news from the world's crop fields in a friendly atmosphere of animated discussion. Guest speakers from the world of crop circle research and beyond regularly give presentations, especially in the winter months. A nominal attendance fee of £1.00 is charged, except for guest speaker evenings which are £2.00. For further details about Southern Circular Research/CCCS Sussex meetings, contact this address:

Southern Circular Research, 44 Meadow Lane, Burgess Hill, West Sussex, RH15 9JA. Tel: 01444 232873

Please note that the details and addresses in these appendices supersede those in ***Fields of Mystery***

CROP CIRCLE PHOTOGRAPHS

Some of the stunning aerial views of crop formations in this book are taken by Steve Alexander, one of the most prolific and professional circle photographers. Copies of photographs, posters and postcards from the last few years are available from Steve. Please send a Stamped Addressed Envelope to the following address and details will be sent to you: **Steve Alexander, 27 St Francis Road, Alverstoke, Gosport, Hampshire, PO12 2UG. Tel: 01705 352867**

APPENDIX 2
BY THE SAME AUTHORS

FIELDS OF MYSTERY:
THE CROP CIRCLE PHENOMENON IN SUSSEX
BY ANDY THOMAS

"Andy Thomas' treatment of a subject for which it is evident he possesses vast conviction and knowledge, makes this book a very enjoyable read indeed" - **UFO Reality** *"An interesting read for anyone not acquainted with the phenomenon and a must for any enthusiasts"* - **Sightings** *"Rich in content and laced with dozens of spectacular photographs"* - **UFO Magazine** *"Well-presented and rational"* - **Encounters** *"A welcome addition in the field of cerealogy… the ground it covers is really a microcosm of a grand design which is resonating all around the world"* - **Nexus**

Two of the major sites for the crop circle phenomenon are the counties of East and West Sussex, which have seen several decades of ongoing activity. *Fields of Mystery* tells the full story of the crop circles of Sussex and the phenomenon world-wide with many fascinating true tales and insights, lavishly illustrated throughout with photographs and diagrams, including a full-colour section.

With a preface by the Rt Hon Denis Healey and a foreword by renowned crop circle researcher Michael Glickman, this book is the ideal companion to *Quest For Contact*. **100 pages, paperback, published by *S B Publications*, ISBN 1 85770 096 1, £6.95**

Copies can be mail ordered from the following address, enclosing a cheque for **£7.95** *(this includes £1.00 extra for p&p) payable to* **'A S Thomas'.** *Overseas orders are* **£8.95** *(to cover p&p). Currency for cheques and POs sent from abroad must be made out in Sterling, drawn on a bank with a British branch:*

Fields of Mystery, 13 Downsview Cottages, Cooksbridge, Lewes, East Sussex, BN8 4TA.

CIRCULAR SUSSEX: *CROP CIRCLES IN SUSSEX* (VIDEO) A VIDEO DOCUMENTARY BY ANDY THOMAS, NARRATED BY PAUL BURA

"The music is an important part of the video and the group manage to capture the mystery of the Sussex season with atmospheric shots of the landscape within the formations, with a bit of humour thrown in for good measure" - **Crop Circle Connector**

In 1993 and 1994, Andy Thomas recorded many Sussex crop formations in detail and the work of the Centre for Crop Circle Studies surveying team. *Circular Sussex*, a half-hour programme professionally edited and presented, documents the appearance of the crop circle phenomenon in Sussex with music by Andy Thomas and David Swingland and narration by Paul Bura. **PAL VHS video cassette, 30 minutes approx, £8.95 (including p&p).**

Copies can be mail ordered from the following address, enclosing a cheque for **£8.95** *(this includes p&p) payable to* **'A S Thomas'**. *Overseas orders are* **£10.95** *(to cover p&p). Currency for cheques and POs sent from abroad must be made out in Sterling, drawn on a bank with a British branch:*

***Circular Sussex*, 13 Downsview Cottages, Cooksbridge, Lewes, East Sussex, BN8 4TA.**

THE OAK ON THE PLAIN: *A MYSTICAL TALE FOR THE ECOLOGICALLY-MINDED* BY PAUL BURA

"Deeply moving. Most poignant. Profound, yet beautiful in its simplicity" - **Liverpool Daily Post & Echo**

'The land was barren... bush and scrub were all that were left of a once proud and thriving community... With outstretched arms the boy seemed to embrace the land. A thrill vibrated through the ground where he stood and for a moment there was a great silence and during that silence the boy drove his staff deep into the summit. Out of his bag of damp moss he took a single acorn...'

So begins an enchanting tale of man and nature and man *as* nature. No-one is too 'grown-up' to read it, and to read it with joy. **28 pages, paperback, published by *Honeytone Promotions*, ISBN 0 9527924 0 0, £2.95.**

Copies can be mail ordered from the following address, enclosing a cheque for **£3.40** *(this includes p&p) payable to* **'Honeytone Promotions'**. *Overseas orders are* **£4.00** *(to cover p&p). Currency for cheques and POs sent from abroad must be made out in Sterling, drawn on a bank with a British branch:*

***The Oak on the Plain*, Honeytone Promotions, Newstead, Instow, Devon, EX39 4LN.**

THE DRUNK ON THE TRAIN *AND OTHER POEMS* BY PAUL BURA

"Paul Bura is a straight down-the-line poet. He is sensitive and emotional, a journalistic poet with a good sense of imagery" - **Spike Milligan** *"I laughed out loud in my midnight room at some of his tough, witty descriptions of childhood, smiled sadly at his love encounters, and groaned when he struck a certain all-too responsive chord within myself. He has a voice that would make Dylan Thomas growl in his grave with envy"* - **Christy Brown**

The Drunk on the Train collects together some of Paul Bura's finest poems, alternately romantic, tragic, touching and roaringly funny. **64 pages, paperback, published by *The Bosgo Press,* ISBN 0 906786 03 7, £4.95.**

Copies can be mail ordered from the following address, enclosing a cheque for **£5.40** *(this includes p&p) payable to* **'Paul Bura'.** *Overseas orders are* **£5.00** *(to cover p&p). Currency for cheques and POs sent from abroad must be made out in Sterling, drawn on a bank with a British branch:*

***The Drunk on the Train,* c/o The Firs, Cemlyn, Nr Cemaes, Anglesey, Gwynedd, LL67 0DU.**

INDEX

THE AUTHORS

ANDY THOMAS

Andy Thomas was born and bred in Lewes, East Sussex, an area he still lives in today with his wife and son.

Andy is editor of the monthly crop circle magazine **SC,** which has a world-wide readership, and is a founder member of the Centre for Crop Circle Studies, Sussex Branch, now Southern Circular Research. He produced a video, *Circular Sussex*, in 1995 and his first book *Fields of Mystery* was released to acclaim in 1996. He has contributed to many different magazines and publications, regularly lectures on crop circles and the unexplained around England and has made several television and radio appearances.

In addition to writing and lecturing, Andy is a professional musician, has composed and recorded for various projects and regularly gigs around south-east England.

PAUL BURA

Paul Bura, broadcaster, poet, writer and 'jobbing psychic', started his career doing many of the voices for Thames Television's *Larry the Lamb* and went on to do countless radio and TV commercial voice-overs. He co-presented BBC Radio 4's *Sounds, Words and Music* and was a reporter (known as 'The Voice') for Channel 4's *Same Difference* programme.

Apart from being a performing artist Paul has seven books of poetry to his credit. He swerved away from poetry with his story *The Oak on the Plain* and then the channelled book *Joeb - Servant of Gaia* (edited by Andy Thomas, currently out of print). Most recently *The Drunk on the Train*, a collection of his finest poems, was published. Paul is currently in the process of moving from Sussex to Anglesey in Wales.

Andy Thomas can be contacted **c/o 13 Downsview Cottages, Cooksbridge, Lewes, East Sussex, BN8 4TA. Tel: 01273 474711**

Paul Bura can be contacted **c/o The Firs, Cemlyn, Nr Cemaes, Anglesey, Gwynedd, LL67 0DU.**